THE MUSICAL MICROCOMPUTER

GARLAND REFERENCE LIBRARY
OF THE HUMANITIES
(VOL. 854)

THE MUSICAL MICROCOMPUTER
A Resource Guide

Craig Lister

GARLAND PUBLISHING, INC. • NEW YORK & LONDON
1988

Library of Congress Cataloging-in-Publication Data

Lister, Craig.
    The musical microcomputer: a resource guide / Craig Lister.
        p. cm. — (Garland reference library of the humanities; vol.
854)
    Includes indexes.
    ISBN 0-8240-8442-X (alk. paper)
    1. Computer music—History and criticism—Bibliography.
2. Microcomputers—Bibliography. I. Title. II. Series.
ML128.C62L57   1988   88–11723
                                                            CIP
                                                            MN

Printed on acid-free, 250-year-life paper
Manufactured in the United States of America

Hail to the IBM

Lift up our proud and loyal voices,
Sing out in accents strong and true,
With hearts and hands to you devoted,
And inspiration ever new;
Your ties of friendship cannot sever,
Your glory time will never stem,
We will toast a name that lives forever,
Hail to the IBM.

Our voices swell in admiration;
Of T. J. Watson proudly sing;
He'll ever be our inspiration,
To him our voices loudly ring;
The IBM will sing the praises,
Of him who brought us world acclaim,
As the volume of our chorus raises,
Hail! To his honored name.[1]

---

[1] From a 1939 songbook of the IBM Corporation, as
found in Dvorak, John C., "Hot Rod Computers,"
Infoworld 7,34 (Aug. 26, 1985): 60. Thomas John Watson
was President, then Chairman of IBM from 1914 to his
death in 1956; he was especially fond of sing-alongs.

Contents

Introduction   ix

I. Bibliography, History, and Criticism   1

II. Composition, Analysis, and Notation   19

III. Education and Musicianship   41

IV. Interfaces: Sequencers, MIDI, Related
    Hardware and Design   71

V. Programming: Languages, Code, Software
    Design, and Artificial Intelligence   95

VI. Synthesis: Acoustics, Voice Editors/
    Libraries, and Sampling   111

Author Index   133

Title and Software Index   147

Appendix A: Journals which Regularly
    Contain Articles on Microcomputer
    Applications in Music   161

Appendix B: A Checklist of Twenty Books for
    the Small Music Library   169

Introduction

This bibliography has been compiled for those interested in microcomputer applications in music. It includes annotated coverage of five types of sources: anthologies, books, dissertations, journal articles, and software. The main organization is by subject, grouped into six composite categories.

Each subject entry has been given a consecutive item number for reference and internal indexing purposes. The two indexes following the subject categories are organized alphabetically by author and title/software. They include the item number reference so that the original annotation and subject category may be located. As appropriate, sources are cross-referenced within the subject index. The aim here has been to bring to the reader's attention those sources which provide substantial information in more than one subject category. Cross-reference is by item number.

Items supplied below were collected with the help of a wide variety of tools. Online computer services provided substantial help, specifically RLIN, ERIC, OCLC, RILM, Magazine Index, Microcomputer Index, Dissertation Abstracts, and Computers and Humanities. Other searches were made through more traditional forms of magazine indexes and library card catalogues. Much of the information concerning software was found in publishers' catalogues, software packages, and commercial bibliographies (i.e., *CODA*, *Mix Bookshelf*, and *Music Education Solutions*). The author's location of materials has been greatly assisted by staffs of the University of Texas, Permian Basin (especially Leslie Fatout and Edward Willman); University of Texas, Austin; Yale Music Library, New Haven; and Library of Congress Music Division, Washington, D.C.

Most of the sources include an annotation, a short statement intended to be descriptive, literal, and accurate. When possible, references to reviews of the source have been included following the annotation. If a source was unavailable, but still seemed relevant, it has been included along with appropriate cautions to the reader. In the case of software, roughly half of the items described in this bibliography were unavailable for inspection. In these cases, I have relied upon reviews and commercial catalogues for classification and annotation.

The goal behind source collection has been to establish a representative, not comprehensive, look at each subject. Many sources were discarded because they were judged irrelevant or out of date. The majority of sources chosen for selection were included because they deal in some substantial way with microcomputer applications in music. A smaller number of items have been included because they deal in a timeless (or transferable) fashion with larger computers, languages, concepts, or histories. The listings provide a wide span of information from introductory to advanced topics, in both theoretical and practical applications. In the specific case of bibliographies, a comprehensive approach has been adopted as these sources allow the reader access to many items not in the immediate scope of this book.

The author was less responsible for deciding subject headings than were the sources themselves. After some fifty books and anthologies had been placed into a database, a variety of keyword designations were developed and applied to individual items. Search procedures on the database made evident an initial list of dominant subjects. As the database grew with the inclusion of journals, dissertations, and software packages--eventually reaching the 336 items given below--subject lists were prepared which showed relationships between categories. If a large amount of cross-referencing was required between two subject areas, then the combination of those subjects was considered. Eventually it was decided that all of the sources could conveniently fit into six composite subject areas.

Guidelines for use

The Musical Microcomputer has been conceived as a gateway to source location and identification. It will serve both those looking for a specific reference and those with a concept or goal in mind.

If you are seeking a specific citation, you may locate it alphabetically by either the author or the title/software indexes. Software items have been formatted as books with the titles in italics and the developers (if known) following the title. Each software citation includes the computer or computers on which it will run at the end. The phrase "series" (e.g., "for Apple II series computers") indicates that all computers in that product name line are suited to the program.

If, instead, you are interested in more general use, such as how music can be notated with a computer, then you should examine the contents page for appropriate subject headings. Under "II. Composition, Analysis, and Notation" you will find software packages for score production, theories about constructing music editors, articles which compare commercially available music editors, and cross-references to related subjects such as "IV. Interfaces." Browsing through the subject index may clarify your question and simplify your goal. Those who use this bibliography as support for a class such as computer applications in music should find these subject indexes of especial help.

One practical way to enter the world of computer languages is to type the code for a program into your microcomputer. Quite a few journals, and a few books, provide such code for musical programs. These are listed in "V. Programming" and provide the prospective "musical hacker" with an avenue for development. Be aware that languages such as BASIC vary from one software company to another and you should locate a program designed specifically for your computer and software language (the prospective programmer is further advised to take an extremely literal approach toward entering code).

If you have just become interested in micro-computers and music, you may wish to subscribe to a magazine which features regularly appearing articles in this field. Appendix A supplies such a list, along with addresses and ordering information. Many of these journals are designed to support specific computers (e.g., *PC Magazine* and *Macworld*) and are not, as a rule, found in public or research libraries. The Library of Congress, Washington, D.C., provides one of the few large collections of these trade journals.

Appendix B supplies a list of twenty books suitable for the small library. These have been chosen because the author is aware of problems associated with developing small music libraries in a highly specialized age. Items have been chosen because they are universal in coverage and/or appeal (Roads and Strawns' anthology, *Foundations of Computer Music,* item 324) or because they fulfill specialized needs exceptionally well (Wittlich, Schafer, and Babb's programming text, *Microcomputers and Music,* item 275). Software items have been excluded from this list as most music libraries are currently unable to process them.

There are many products and software packages in the microcomputer world which are not compatible with each other. Often the annotations herein speak to the need for an ancillary item ("DAC board required," "requires MIDI hardware interface"). Before purchasing any item, you should check with your local supplier to make sure it will do what you wish it to.

As evidenced by software and program design, the most popular microcomputers at this date are Amiga, Apple II series, Atari ST, Commodore 64/128, IBM PC series, Macintosh, and Radio Shack Tandy series. Musical items for all of these computers are found in the listings below. Information concerning the microcomputers themselves, however, has not been included. Considering the astounding rate at which hardware continues to develop, it seemed most appropriate to refer the reader to his or her computer dealer. Fortunately, manufacturers are now making some attempt at compatibility when designing a new product line.

It is a popular adage that you should buy a computer which will run the specific software packages you need. This is especially true in the case of music software. Do not assume that a popular music editor designed for computer X will soon become available for computer Y. Even if the developer so desired, there are internal hardware constraints which can make such a transference impossible.

When available, prices have been appended to the citations. These are particularly important in the case of software as these packages may be quite expensive and the relative cost of a program often is an indication of its sophistication. All prices are current as of 1988 and are, of course, subject to change.

The MIDI revolution and labeling of software packages

In 1983, a select number of manufacturers who had been interfacing musical instruments with computers recognized the need for a standard of information transference. A MIDI (=Musical Instrument Digital Interface) standard was established so hardware and software designers could ensure compatibility amongst diverse products (cf. item 33 below). Instruments, especially synthesizers, began "talking" to computers and computers began "talking" back.

The MIDI revolution represents a last hardware step in an evolution designed to provide the musician with a superb creative tool. In a practical sense, the computer can now control the complete musical cycle of play, notate, edit, analyze, print, and play once again. Synthesizers make it possible for anyone with rudimentary keyboard skills to input music rapidly into a sequencer, quantization makes it possible to turn these signals into a musical score, and onscreen editing procedures make it efficient for composers, performers, and musicologists to manipulate their material. The result may then be printed in score format for traditional performance or moved back into the sequencer for electronic realization (for detailed information on this procedure, see items 193-196).

From 1985 on the hardware and software which makes this cycle possible has been available for popular microcomputers. Musicians worldwide have found one use after another for the technology (this author spends a good amount of time editing 18th-century symphonies with just such a tool). The technology is particularly worthy for it allows a substantial amount of flexibility depending upon the software packages employed. Editors, sequencers, and musicianship programs have dominated so far, but there is no reason why analytical, historical, and creative programs should not soon rival their predecessors.

Once the MIDI standard was in place, software designers began expanding the musical role of microcomputers and certain categories of software packages began to coalesce. In particular, four types of programs have now become available for most micro-computers: sequencers, editors, samplers, and voice libraries. For the musician not familiar with these packages, the following definitions are supplied.

Sequencers: software programs which record input from a MIDI instrument into a computer. A typical MIDI setup implies a keyboard synthesizer connected to your computer by means of the serial port (requiring a hardware adapter). Once you have input music into a sequencer program, you may then play and edit the series at will. The number of voices which may be combined and the flexibility and ease of editing procedures are dependent upon the particular software package; in all cases, a MIDI data stream allows for a maximum of sixteen channels at the interface stage. Some sequencers allow for a process called "quantization," in which the signal is adjusted to conform to attack and release determinants. Quantization is necessary should you wish to transfer sequencer data into a music editor.

Editors: software programs which notate and edit musical scores. Musicians might think of these programs as the musical equivalent of a word processor; they manipulate musical symbols in a fashion similar to the way words are manipulated. The best music editors offer easy inputting and flexible editing characteristics. One great advantage of MIDI instruments is that with an appropriate sequencer and MIDI hardware connection, you may input scores directly into your computer from any MIDI instrument. This procedure offers tremendous savings in time when compared to older forms of coded entry by means of the QWERTY keyboard. Most editors will support dot-matrix printers and some will support laser printers. For desktop publishing purposes, the latter is an expensive requirement.

Samplers: software programs which sample analog waveforms and provide a digital representation for storing, editing, and playback purposes. Samplers may be used to create electronic representations of acoustic instruments or to filter and otherwise edit any analog representation. In some cases the digitized waveform may be played back through a sampler with synthesizer capabilities (such as the *Ensoniq Mirage*) or stored in a voice library.

   Voice Editors/Libraries: software programs which store, organize, and edit digital waveform patterns.   One of the benefits of linking a computer to a musical instrument is the rapidity with which the computer can recall complicated waveform representations and transmit them to a synthesizer.   Voice libraries allow for a vast number of timbres to be stored for editing and recall purposes.   Onscreen editing allows for visual representations of the waveform and accompanying sound characteristics such as attack and decay.   Some manufacturers have taken the further step of supplying sound libraries of prerecorded timbres encompassing everything from sound effects to full orchestral forces.

   In this bibliography, music editors are found in "II. Composition, Analysis, and Notation," MIDI products and sequencers in "IV. Interfaces," and samplers and voice libraries in "VI. Synthesis."   Once again, the cautions made above concerning compatibility should be heeded. Despite the MIDI standard, many products are designed for only one microcomputer.   You should select a MIDI hardware interface and accompanying software with great care, and in conjunction with your local dealer, in order to ensure proper performance.

The sources in general and future speculations

   For the layperson, early sources about computers and music can be a terrifying thing.   Full of mathematical and engineering terms, acronyms and jargon, these sources describe the acoustical side of a complex art (music) as it might be used or represented by a technical machine (the computer).   Much early work was devoted to solving technical problems, considering the theoretical nature of the computer as a creative, research, and education tool, and in developing languages for compositional, performance, and notational purposes.

Once the microcomputer began making its impact on American society in the 1970s, musicians began taking a more practical approach toward computer usage. Educators employed microcomputers for classroom experiments and testing, scholars considered ways of analyzing and authenticating music by microanalytical and statistical methods, theorists began developing software packages for notation and musicianship, and on and on (the list is fleshed out by the rest of this book).

By 1981, David Shrader was able to claim "the microcomputer revolution in music instruction has already occurred and it is only now a matter of time before it permeates all levels of instruction (see item 164 below)." Shrader's statement is both prophetic and problematic. While microcomputers have certainly found an important niche in classroom use, the quality of software and resulting teaching efficiency is still being evaluated (cf. items 112, 116, 157, and 176).

The most practical and pervasive trend documented by this bibliography concerns the MIDI revolution described above. Once this standard became a reality, the entire musical world could participate in computer applications on whatever creative level they chose. As a composition, performance, and timbral tool, the microcomputer/synthesizer chain offers a vast wealth of possibilities which could well occupy musicians for many decades. Now that musical data may easily be encoded into sequencer/editor programs, it seems reasonable to assume that new software packages will soon arise. Analytical programs would be particularly useful (these have already been developed in some sophistication for non-MIDI computers, see item 66), as would a new generation of musicianship and education tutors that stress flexibility and increased instructor control (see item 176).

An important lesson to be learned from the success of MIDI is that by standardizing the tools involved, all aspects of the technology are available to the culture. The process could be extended to other parts of the computer realm. For some years, computer scientists have been active in pursuing a language which will admit artificial intelligence. An early prototype (PROLOG) has already reached the marketplace.

To simplify, scientists are searching for a computer language high enough so that the computer can make decisions and write its own code for operation. The latter step is now a reality in certain fields and with certain large computers and languages (notably LISP). Once again, a software revolution is on the horizon.

This new revolution would require that musicians, linguists, engineers, and computer specialists work together to agree on what a musical language might be (see items 247 and 270 for nascent studies in this area). Now that rapid input of scores into microcomputers is a reality, we are faced with a tremendous source of information in an exceptionally malleable form. The only restrictions on manipulating the data will be our imaginations and our understanding of musical processes.

Craig Lister

The Musical Microcomputer

I. Bibliography,
History, and Criticism

1. Bahler, Peter B. "Electronic and Computer Music: an Annotated Bibliography of Writings in English." MA Thesis, Eastman School of Music. Ann Arbor: UMI Press, 1966. vii, 128pp.

   Not available for review.

2. Bartle, Barton K. *Computer Software in Music and Music Education: A Guide.* Metuchen, N.J.: Scarecrow Press, 1988. xiv, 252pp. 0810820560.

   To be released in early 1988.

3. Battier, M., with J. Arveiller. *Musique et Informatique: Une Bibliographie Indexée.* Paris: Département Musique: Université Paris, VIII, 1976. 172pp.

   List of 1485 items arranged alphabetically by author. Coverage spans all western languages with English sources predominating. Each entry is provided with a topic code(s); a subject index at the end groups sources according to their content.

Listings include software and program
languages. Indexes supplied as acronym
tables, key subject words, program names
(GROOVE, MUSCOR, etc.), and list of languages.

4. Boody, Charles G. "Non-Compositional Applications
of the Computer to Music: An Evaluative Study of
Materials Published in America Through June of
1972." Ph.D. dissertation, University of Minnesota.
Ann Arbor: UMI Press, 1975. vii, 186pp.

A review of computer materials prior to
1974 in the following categories: music
input, thematic indices and printing,
computer assisted analysis, and "complete"
systems. Concludes with an "immodest
proposal" for standardizing hardware,
software, musical languages, and research
facilities. Bibliography.

5. Brook, Barry S., Ed. *Musicology and the Computer:
Musicology 1966-2000: A Practical Program. Three
Symposia.* New York: The City University of New
York Press, 1970. x, 275pp. 73-152570.

Three symposia dealing with conceptual
issues of basic importance in employing
computers for musicological research.
Symposium I considers analytical topics,
II, input languages necessary for repre-
senting music, and III, new directions and
utopian proposals. Discussion and com-
mentary follow each symposium. Extensive bibliography of 617 items grouped
into seven categories, index.

6. Carlsen, J., and D. Williams. *A Computer Annotated Bibliography: Music Research in Programmed Instruction 1952-1972*. Reston, Va.: Music Educators National Conference Publication, 1978. 71pp. 77-50341.

> An annotated index of 51 studies devoted to CAI topics. Listings are organized alphabetically by author and include annotations (a literal explanation of topics such as "content area," "academic level," "program objectives," "presentations mode," etc.). Coverage emphasizes doctoral dissertations and articles from educational journals. Supplies an interesting "taxonomy of topics-subtopics developed for annotating music research in programed instruction," and accompanying index by these topic areas.

--- Clynes, Manfred, ed. *Music, Mind, and Brain: The Neuropsychology of Music*. New York: Plenum Press, 1982. xii, 430pp. 0306409089.

> Articles of vast interdisciplinary scope; see main entry no. 252.

7. *CODA–The New Music Software Catalog*. Owatonna, Minn.: Wenger Corp., 1986. 160pp. $4.00.

> An extravagantly produced commercial bibliography of software sources for Apple II, Commodore, Macintosh, IBM, Atari, and Amiga computers. Grouped into six major sections by computer, *C O D A* employs subtopics (music printing, voice librarians, sequencing and recording, etc.) to organize software. Appendices

supplied as MIDI interfaces, accessories, videos, and books. An excellent source for both browsing and ordering specific software items. Originally intended as a yearly publication, the firm has now shifted their emphasis from retailing to publishing and plans no further catalogues.

8. *Composers and Their Works* (developed by D. Williams, A. Blackford, and B. Kliment). Bellevue, Wash.: Temporal Acuity Products, Inc., ca. 1980. (for Apple II series computers): $70.00.

A CAD software program in which the user identifies, spells, or recalls the name of a composer or his work. Composers and compositions are grouped into eighteen nationalities and six style periods.

9. Cross, Lowell. *A Bibliography of Electronic Music.* Toronto: University of Toronto Press, 1967, 1970. Reprint by Ann Arbor: UMI Press, 1987. ix, 126pp. 0802014348.

A bibliography of 1563 sources encompassing five main topics: "musique concrète," electronic music, tape music, computer music, and experimental music. Includes coverage of English, German, French, and other European sources prior to 1966. No annotations, but indexed according to topic and author.

10. Davis, Deta S. "Computer Applications in Music: A Bibliography" (Proceedings of the 1980 International Computer Music Conference). San

Francisco, Calif.: Computer Music Association
Publications, 1981. Pages 653-824. $58.00.

Listing of 1202 sources alphabetically by
author.   Employs seventeen categories
(aesthetics, analysis, Braille printing,
composition, composers, CAI, conferences,
electronic and pipe organs, music
industry, printing and transcription,
musicology, psychology and psycho-
acoustics, record restoration, reference
and research, software, sound generation
with subtopics, and miscellaneous) offer-
ing exceptionally thorough coverage.   The
author is currently publishing an ex-
panded version of 4585 items as *Computer
Applications in Music: A Bibliography*
(Madison, Wis.: A-R Editions, 1988).   Davis's
update is designed to be comprehensive as
of mid-1986.

11. Donato, Peter. "Writers Turn Computer into Modern
Age Muse; Composers Say Computers Can Up
Creativity Once Mastered." *The Canadian Composer*,
218 (Feb.-March 1987): 10-14.

Descriptions of the microcomputer
activities of Bruce Fowler (film, theatre,
and industrial soundtracks), Scott Merritt
(guitarist and composer), Allan Guttman
(composer and arranger), and Paul
Hoffert (film composer and professor of
electronic music).

12. Eddins, John M. "A Brief History of Computer-
Assisted Instruction in Music." *College Music
Symposium*, 21,2 (Fall 1981): 7-14.

A summary of CAI techniques from 1967 to 1979 supported liberally with quotes from educational studies.

--- Foerster, H., and J. Beauchamp, eds. *Music by Computers*. New York: John Wiley and Sons, Inc., 1969. xv, 139pp. 69-19244.

See article on imperfection in computer music by Strang, main entry no. 255.

13. *Foreign Instrument Names* (developed by D. Williams, A. Blackford, and B. Kliment). Bellevue, Wash.: Temporal Acuity Products, Inc., ca. 1980. (for Apple II series computers): $50.00.

A CAD software program for teaching foreign term identification. Instrument names are provided in French, German, and Italian.

14. *General Music Terms* (developed by D. Williams, A. Blackford, and J. Schulze). Bellevue, Wash.: Temporal Acuity Products, Inc., ca. 1980. (for Apple II series computers): $70.00.

A CAD software program for instruction in general term recognition. Supplies common terms in melodic, harmonic, formal, stylistic, and other theoretical areas.

15. Hewlett, W., and E. Selfridge-Field. *Directory of Computer Assisted Research in Musicology*. Menlo Park, Calif.: Center for Computer Assisted Research in the Humanities Park (Yearly Serial), 1985. 56pp.

86-101572; 1986. 86pp. 0936943017; 1987. 151pp. (No ISBN available.)

Yearly directory of computer applications in musicology. The *Directory* is produced by questionnaire with feature articles of current interest. Found in the 1986 issue are I, the current state of music printing by computer along with hardware and software descriptions and examples, II, a bibliography including indices of text, indices of music, databases of text, databases and editions of music, text analysis, music analysis and analytical methods, III, selected literature, and IV, the addresses of individuals, agencies, and companies.

16. *Italian Terms* (developed by D. Williams, A. Blackford, and B. Kliment). Bellevue, Wash.: Temporal Acuity Products, Inc., ca. 1980. (for Apple II series computers): $50.00.

A CAD software program providing instruction in term recognition. The user defines Italian terms in multiple choice format.

17. Kostka, Stefan M. *A Bibliography of Computer Applications in Music* (Music Indexes and Bibliographies, No. 7). Hackensack, N.J.: J. Boonin, 1974. iii, 58pp. 0913574074.

Listing of 641 items arranged alphabetically by author. Entries exhibit an exceptionally high degree of accuracy and care as regards selection. The work includes references to reviews and abstracts

but no annotations.   An essential resource
guide for sources prior to 1974.

18. Krepack, B., and R. Firestone. *Start Me Up! The
Music Biz Meets the Personal Computer.* Van Nuys,
Calif.: Mediac Press, 1986. xvii, 171pp. 0961644605.
$12.95.

An excellent introduction into the use of
microcomputers for popular and commercial musicians.   Written in a casual
and engaging style, categories such as
office use, modems, accounting procedures, touring, publicity, and actual
musical production are presented in a dual
format: first as explanatory text, then
with reinforcing examples taken from
real life industry (="Connections").   The
latter offer a mine of information for the
practical musician, especially those
oriented toward business applications.
Three appendices as glossary, quick
answers to a few frequently asked
questions, and the music biz/computer
resource and contact list.

19. Lavroff, Nicholas. "The Software Rock 'n' Roll
Band." *Macworld,* 2,11 (Nov. 1985): 114-119.

Provides historical and biographical
information on the three developers of
MacroMind, a software company: Marc
Cantor, Jay Fenton, and Mark Pierce.

20. Leibs, Albert S. "Music & the Microchip:

Instruments Get User Friendly: Today's Technology Could Bring Out the Mozart in You." *Information WEEK*, 128 (Aug. 3, 1987): 18-21.

A broad consideration of recent trends in computer applications in music. Supplies viewpoints by Frank Zappa, Robert Moog, William Brinkley, and others on current usage and future speculations.

21. Lincoln, Harry B., ed. *The Computer and Music*. Ithaca, N.Y.: Cornell University Press, 1970. 354pp. 0801405505.

Anthology containing an excellent history of computers to 1970 (Edmund Bowles) followed by selected articles on composition, analysis, ethnomusicology, musicology, and information handling and retrieval. *The Computer and Music* defines general themes well and offers a useful first look at major avenues of computer applications.

22. Mancini, J., and P. Freiberger. "European Computer Music Research Challenges American Efforts." *Popular Computing*, 4,6 (April 1985): 22.

Report on the October, 1985 Annual International Music Conference with succinct descriptions of the activities of IRCAM (Institute for Research in Acoustics and Music), GRM (Musical Research Group), CEMAMu (Center for the Study of Mathematics and Automated Music), and CSC (Center for Computer Sonology). Includes brief descriptions of the hardware employed by each organization.

--- Manning, Peter. "Computers and Music Composition." *Proceedings of the Royal Musical Association,* 107 (1980-1981): 119-131.

An article on composition with impressive historical breadth; see main entry no. 65.

23. Manning, Peter. *Electronic and Computer Music.* Oxford: Clarendon Press, 1985. 291pp. 0193119188. $29.95.

A descriptive and historically oriented account of electronic and computer trends from 1945 to 1980. Contains a detailed analysis of Schaeffer's "musique con-crète," early procedures of tone synthesis in Cologne, and description of the development of the RCA synthesizer in America. Other chapters consider voltage-controlled synthesis, works for tape (with or without accompanying performers), live electronic music, rock and pop electronic music, and computer music. Concludes with appendices, bibliography, discography, and index.

Review:
Byte, 11,6 (June 1986): 76.

24. Mathews, M., and F. Moore. "Computers and Future Music." *Science,* 183,4122 (Jan. 25, 1974): 263-268.

A discussion of two early and important systems for composition and performance,

Music V and Groove. Concludes with "Musical Futures," an extraordinarily accurate prediction of its day (1974) for upcoming trends. Bibliography.

25. McConkey, Jim. "Report on the Third Annual Symposium on Small Computers in the Arts." *Computer Music Journal*, 8,2 (Summer 1984): 41-47.

Description of papers read at the Third Small Computer Symposium, Philadelphia, 1983.

26. McConkey, Jim. "The Second Annual Symposium on Small Computers in the Arts." *Computer Music Journal*, 7,3 (Fall 1983): 25-30.

Description of papers read at the Second Small Computer Symposium, held on October 15-17, 1982 at Philadelphia.

27. Melby, Carol. *Computer Music Compositions of the United States*, 2nd ed. (First International Conference on Computer Music at Illinois). Cambridge, Mass.: MIT Press, 1976. 28pp. 78-305572.

A slim but useful volume providing a non-inclusive list of computerized compositions prior to 1976. Listings include composers' names and addresses along with categories scoring, score availability, recording, tape, duration, and hardware requirements. Melby's work is oriented toward mainframe devices but many of these programs could now be run on larger micros. Appendices as lists of record companies and publishers.

28. *Music Symbols.* (developed by D. Williams, A. Blackford, and J. Schulze). Bellevue, Wash.: Temporal Acuity Products, Inc., ca. 1980. (for Apple II series computers): $70.00.

> A CAD software program for instruction in symbol recognition; contains two skill levels.

29. *Music Terminology.* Electronic Courseware Systems, n.d. (for IBM PC, Apple II series, Commodore 64 computers): $39.95.

> A CAD software program with exercises for term identification. The program is based on a glossary of 48 terms excerpted from the *Harvard Dictionary of Music.*

30. Patton, P., and A. Holoien. *Computing in the Humanities* (Lexington Book Series in Computer Science). Lexington, Mass.: Lexington Books, 1981. xi, 401pp. 0669033979.

> Not available for review.

31. *Peter and the Wolf.* Educational Audio Visual, Inc., 1984. (for Commodore 64 and Apple II series computers): $39.95.

> A CAI software program which teaches theme identification to the young. Includes a test for choosing the specific theme associated with a given character and a clever contest between Peter and the Wolf.

32. Peters, G., and J. Eddins. "Applications of Computers to Music Pedagogy, Analysis, and Research: A Selected Bibliography." *Journal of Computer-Based Instruction,* 5,1-2 (Aug. and Nov. 1978): 41-44.

A bibliography of 104 articles, conference proceedings, project reports, dissertations, books, and "research in progress," which examine pedagogical topics. No annotations.

33. Powell, Roger. "The Challenge of Music Software: An Overview of the Current State of Computers in Music." *Byte,* 11,6 (June 1986): 145-150.

General overview of MIDI applications placed in historical context. Provides a good first reading for the musician interested in MIDI.

34. *Proceedings of the International Computer Music Conference.* San Francisco, Calif.: Computer Music Association Publications, 1975 to date.

Yearly papers of the International Computer Music Conference. The *Proceedings* currently available are 1975 at Illinois, 1977 at San Diego, 1978 at Chicago, 1980 at New York, 1981 at Denton, Tex., 1982 at Venice, 1983 at Rochester, 1984 at Paris, 1985 at Vancouver, 1986 at The Hague. Many volumes contain bibliographies; all consider recent and seminal research in computer/music applications.

--- Roads, Curtis, ed. *Composers and the Computer* (The

Computer Music and Digital Audio Series). Los Alto, Calif.: William Kaufmann, Inc., 1984. xxi, 201. 0865760853.

> Introduction by Roads and interviews with Dashow and Lewis contain important historical information; see main entry no. 80.

--- Roads, Curtis. "Research in Music and Artificial Intelligence." *ACM Computing Surveys*, 17,2 (June, 1985): 163-190.

> Superb introduction into artificial intelligence and history of "intelligent machines"; see main entry no. 270.

--- Roads, C., and J. Strawn, eds. *Foundations of Computer Music*. Cambridge, Mass.: MIT Press, 1985 (hardback), 1987 (paperback). xiii, 712pp. 0262181142(h), 0262680513(p).

> "Foreword" and "Overviews" contain historical perspectives; see main entry no. 324.

--- Shrader, David L. "Microcomputer-Based Teaching: Computer-Assisted Instruction of Music Comes of Age." *College Music Symposium*, 21,2 (Fall 1981): 27-36.

> Statement of the role of microcomputers in education, ca. 1980; see main entry no. 164.

35. *Standard Instrument Names* (developed by D.

Williams, A. Blackford, and J. Schulze). Bellevue, Wash.: Temporal Acuity Products, Inc., ca. 1980. (for Apple II series computers): $50.00.

A CAD software program providing instruction in instrument name recognition. Supplies drills for common orchestral and popular instruments with beginning and advanced skill levels.

36. Stein, Evan. *Use of Computers in Folklore and Folk Music: A Preliminary Bibliography* (intact Occasional Papers, No. 1). Los Angeles, Calif.: University of Southern California, School of Performing Arts, 1979. 12pp.

Listing of 115 items arranged alphabetically by author (no annotations or numbering system). Includes coverage of many languages with numerous citations from central Europe. Prepared originally as a Library of Congress guide for the Archive of Folk Culture.

37. Storey, Cheryl E. "A Bibliography of Computer Music" (Proceedings of the International Computer Music Conference at NTSU). Denton, Tex.: North Texas State University Music Library, 1981. 41pp.

A selective bibliography of some 500 items published by the Music Library of North Texas State University for the International Computer Music Conference, November 5-8, 1981. Sources grouped alphabetically according to categories I, periodicals, II, books and studies, III, scores, IV, discography, and V, articles. No annotations but includes call numbers for

North Texas State library holdings in the
left margins.

38. The, Lee. "The Music Connection: Even if You Can't
   Read or Write Music, Your Computer Can." *Personal
   Computing*, 10,1 (Jan. 1986): 89-95.

   Descriptions of microcomputer usage by
   popular musicians Jim Segel, Jim
   Gardiner, and Anthony Scelba. Applications include studio, recording, and
   performance use.

39. Tjepkema, Sandra L. *A Bibliography of Computer
   Music: A Reference for Composers*. Iowa City, Iowa:
   University of Iowa Press, 1981. xvii, 276pp.
   0877451109.

   Annotated listing of 1017 sources
   including books, articles, dissertations,
   papers, and users manuals. Emphasizes
   composition sources which are catalogued
   into five areas: notation, performance,
   creative processes aided by programming,
   digital synthesis, and programmed
   controls. Covers all European languages
   with pre-1981 dates. Concludes with a
   brief list of acronyms, manufacturers'
   addresses, and indexes by subject and
   name.

   Review:
   Computer Music Journal, 5,4 (Winter
   1981): 76.

40. Upitis, Rena. "Milestones in Computer Music

Instruction." *Music Educators Journal*, 69,5 (Jan. 1983): 40-42.

Brief, historical summary of CAI techniques from the late-1960s to 1982. Suggests that "computers are being regarded less as a vehicle for delivering programmed instruction and more as a means for allowing children to actively manipulate variables and solve problems (p. 41)."

41. "US Festival." *Microcomputing*, 6,11 (Nov. 1982): 98-101.

Account of the US Festival (Sept. 3-5, 1982, San Bernadino, Calif.) held to showcase rock music and new computer technology.

42. Victor, Michele. "L'Informatique musicale." *Musique en Jeu*, 18 (April 1975): 45-62.

Report on the activities of major computer figures in the mid-1970s. Topics include composition with Xenakis, analysis with Greussay, Leipp, and Barbaud, and synthesis with Mathews and Risset. Concludes with a model plan for a utopian synthesizer.

43. Wolfe, George. "Creative Computers--Do They 'Think'?" *Music Educators Journal*, 69,5 (Jan. 1983): 59-62.

A broad based consideration of artistic creativity contrasted with a specific computer model designed to compose melodies. Concludes, in part, "If indeed a computer can be made to produce acceptable compositions . . . then the mechanics of lower-order creativity clearly can be taught (p. 62)."

44. Yavelow, Christopher. "Top of the Charts: On Stage and in the Studio, the Mac Is Number One with Music Professionals." *Macworld*, 4,8 (Aug. 1987): 138-145.

Excellent coverage of Macintosh computer usages in sound design, performance, film scoring, and opera arenas. Graphic depictions of model studios offer a quick introduction into Macintosh hardware selection. The specific studios of Frank Serafine, Alan Howarth, Bryan Bell, and Pat Hollenback illustrate practical approaches toward studio design.

45. Young, Jeffrey S. "Peerless Itzhak Perlman." *Macworld*, 2,6 (June 1985): 160-163.

A conversation with Itzhak Perlman on computer and related topics.

II. Composition, Analysis, and Notation

--- Abbott, G., and C. Loy. "Programming Languages for Computer Music Synthesis, Performance, and Composition." *ACM Computing Surveys*, 17,2 (June 1985): 235-262.

> Includes discussion of languages for notation and composition; see main entry no. 247.

46. Baroni, M., and L. Callegari, eds. *Musical Grammars and Computer Analysis* (Quaderni della Rivista italia di musicologia, v. 8). Florence: Leo Olschki, 1984. 374pp. 8822232291.

> Not available for inspection.

47. Bateman, Wayne. *Introduction to Computer Music* (A Wiley-Interscience Publication). N.Y.: John Wiley and Sons., 1980. vii, 314pp. 0471052663. $20.00.

> A traditional introduction into computer usage for the serious musician interested in composition. Opens with introductory topics of I, acoustical concepts, II, tone generation, III, modulation and dynamics,

IV, wave-form analysis, and V, synthesis
of complex tones.   Major   sections   on
composition include I, modification and
processing   of   recorded   sounds,   II,
simulation and reproduction of natural
sounds, III, scales and tonality, as well as
more general discussions of compositional
procedures (presented as set analogies)
and human creativity (understood as an
organic   process).   Appendixes offer a
glossary and two valuable sections on
programming in, respectively, BASIC and
FORTRAN.   Bibliography at the end of each
chapter.

48. Bent, I., and J. Morehen. "Computers in the Analysis
    of Music. *Proceedings of the Royal Musical
    Association*, 104 (1977-1978): 30-46.

    An introduction to computer logic with
    analysis of two compositions by computer
    means.   Authors employ language SPITBOL
    to check for formal divisions and repe-
    titions in a three-voice organum by
    Perotin ("Benedicamus Domino") and lan-
    guage FORTRAN for detecting errors in
    16th-century text underlay.

49. Blombach, Ann K. "A Conceptual Framework for the
    Use of the Computer in Music Analysis." Ph.D.
    dissertation, Ohio State University, Ann Arbor: UMI
    Press, 1976. vi, 340pp.

    A broad based assessment of techniques
    and problems associated with comput-
    erized analysis. Emphasizes secondary
    sources and preexisting software.
    Considers many methods for computer-

aided style analysis and concludes, in part "to achieve their analytic goals . . . musicians need the support of a conceptual framework--a broad understanding of all aspects of computer-aided analysis (p. 269)." Appendices as data preparation, computer instructions/output, utilization of results, and bibliography.

50. Brantley, Daniel L. "Disputed Authorship of Musical Works: A Quantitative Approach to the Attribution of the Quartets Published as Haydn's Opus 3." Ph.D. dissertation, University of Iowa. Ann Arbor: UMI Press, 1977. v, 92pp.

Examines the authorship of the Opus 3 *Quartets* of Haydn/Hoffstetter by a quantitative analysis of micro-elements. Surveys analytical techniques in literature as a parallel to musical analysis and then employs six programs for manipulation of data (RESTORE, VERIFY, ARRAYNGE, ANALYZE, AFFINITY, and SAS/76--DISCRM). Concludes there is a 79% probability Hoffstetter wrote the eleven fast movements of the set, a 50% probability he composed the s l o w movements. Suggests improvements for discriminant analysis. Appendices as flow charts for five programs (no code) and bibliography.

51. Byrd, Donald A. "Musical Notation by Computer." Ph.D. dissertation, Indiana University. Ann Arbor: UMI Press, 1984. xvii, 238pp.

Studies problems, techniques, concepts,
and programs associated with the printing
of conventional music notation. Outlines
the considerable graphic problems
connected with musical symbols and their
placement and the relationship of these
symbols to concepts of artificial intelligence. Concludes artificial intelligence
levels are not nearly advanced enough to
accomplish meaningful notational tasks
(as of 1984) and suggests input ease must
be sacrificed in favor of accurate output.
Offers a System for MUsic Transcription
(=SMUT) which supports polyphony and
shared staves. Appendix I details SMUT as
a thorough user's guide. Excellent bibliography.

52. Campbell, Philip. "The Music of Digital Computers."
Nature, 324,6097 (Dec. 1986): 523-528.

Analysis of two recent compositions
produced by IRCAM composers, Harvey's
Mortuos Plango, Vivos Voco and Boulez's
Répons. Considers I, technological requirements, II, musical structure, and III,
synthesis and performance techniques for
each work. A pacesetting example of
music analysis for modern computer
compositions.

--- Clough, John. "TEMPO: a Composer's Programming
Language." *Perspectives of New Music*, 9,1 (1970):
113-125.

Explanation of TEMPO, a composer's
language; see main entry no. 251.

53. *ConcertWare+*. Stanford, Calif.: Great Wave Software, 1985. (for Macintosh computers): $69.95.

Three programs in a single software package which compose, print, and synthesize sounds on Macintosh computers. Music entry by keyboard or mouse in early version, "keyboard" version uses a non-MIDI keyboard and "MIDI" version interconnects with any MIDI instrument.

Reviews:
A+, 3,10 (Oct. 1985): 132-138.
Byte, 11,6 (June 1986): 273-276.
Nibble, 6,8 (Aug. 1985): 122-130.
Macworld, 2,6 (June 1985): 72-79.
Macworld, 3,12 (Dec. 1986): 109-117.
Computer Music Journal, 9,3 (Fall 1985): 52-67.

54. *Deluxe Music Construction Set*. San Mateo, Calif.: Electronic Arts, 1985. (for Macintosh computers): $49.95.

An inexpensive music editor with MIDI potential and good printing support (dot-matrix, laser, and *Sonata* font). You may input music by keyboard, mouse, or MIDI instrument, the latter in conjunction with sequencers *MegaTrack* (item 215), or *MIDIMac* (item 220).

Reviews:
Macworld, 3,2 (Feb. 1986): 93-99.
Electronic Learning, 4,8 (May/June 1985): 45-47.
Macworld, 3,12 (Dec. 1986): 109-117.

55. Dodge, C., and C. Bahn. "Musical Fractals:
Mathematical Formulas Can Produce Musical as Well
as Graphic Fractals." *Byte,* 11,6 (June 1986): 185-196.

Important introduction into the use of
fractal geometry for music and graphic
use. Includes BASIC programs for creating white, Brownian, and fractional
noises as well as two programs which
produce and play music created by
fractals. Programs written for Yamaha CX
5-M computer; may be altered for most
other BASIC languages and hardwares.

56. Dodge, C., and T. Jerse. *Computer Music: Synthesis,
Composition, and Performance.* N.Y.: Schirmer
Books, 1985. xi, 383pp. 002873100X.

Classic text suitable for a graduate course
in computer music. Includes background
information on computers, languages,
software, and acoustics; detailed consideration of synthesis techniques, sound-
processing techniques, composition, and
real-time performance. Offers an
excellent chapter on speech synthesis and
a useful appendix "Synthesis Algorthms"
(written in FORTRAN). References are at
the end of each chapter; concludes with a
glossary and index of names/terms.

Review:
Byte, 11,6 (June 1986): 67-70.

--- Foerster, H., and J. Beauchamp, eds. *Music by
Computers.* N.Y.: John Wiley and Sons, Inc., 1969. xv,
139pp. 69-19244.

Articles on algorithms in composition; see main entry no. 255.

57. Glines, Jeffrey. "Mac Toots Its Own Horn." *Macworld*, 2,5 (May 1985): 33.

Describes compositional uses of the Macintosh computer by David Kelsey and Ted Lane.

58. Gomberg, David A. "A Computer-Oriented System for Music Printing." D.Sc. dissertation, Washington University. Ann Arbor: UMI Press, 1975. vi, 120pp.

Theoretical development and description of a music printing system for traditional music which employs DARMS input and PL/1 programming language. Eliot Carter's *Double Concerto* is used as a model for input and symbolic problems. Considers the impact of computerized techniques on the music publishing industry and concludes that computerized systems are more cost effective than traditional notational methods. Appendices offer canonic DARMS BNF specifications, notes for future implementors, and a bibliography.

--- Gourlay, John S. "A Language for Music Printing." *Communications of the ACM*, 29,5 (May 1986): 388-401.

See main entry no. 258.

59. Gross, Dorothy S. "A Set of Computer Programs to

Aid in Music Analysis." Ph.D. dissertation, Indiana
University. Ann Arbor: UMI Press, 1975. vi, 358pp.

The development of six analytical
programs which explore pattern tracing,
grouping of sonorities, thematic analysis,
harmonic analysis, set analysis, and
melodic and harmonic lists. Uses the
language CAL SNOBOL with a CDC 6600
computer. A sample analysis is based on
Dallapiccola's *Quaderno Musicale*, No. 11.
Offers appendices as scores, user's manual,
results, programs, and bibliography.

60. Heid, Jim. "Musical Wares." *Macworld,* 3,2 (Feb.
1986): 92-99.

Introduction to computerized score
production using the Macintosh computer.
Comparative analysis of ten software
packages: *Deluxe Music Construction Set*
(item 54), *Professional Composer* (item 76),
ConcertWare (item 53), *Keyboard, MIDI,
MusicWorks 512K* (item 72), *Total Music,
StudioMac, MIDIMac* (item 220), *MegaTrack*
(item 215), and *MIDI Composer*. Addresses
and prices provided for all software.

--- Hewlett W., and E. Selfridge-Field. *Directory of
Computer Assisted Research in Musicology.* Menlo
Park, Calif.: Center for Computer Assisted Research
in the Humanities (Yearly Serial), 1985 on.

Yearly review of music editors; see main
entry no. 15.

61. Jackson, David L. "Horizontal and Vertical Analysis

Data Extraction Using a Computer Program." Ph.D. dissertation, University of Cincinnati. Ann Arbor: UMI Press, 1981. 423 pp.

Not available for inspection.

62. Kolosick, J. Timothy. "A Computer-Assisted, Set-Theoretic Investigation of Vertical Simultaneities in Selected Piano Compositions by Charles E. Ives." Ph.D. dissertation, University of Wisconsin-Madison. Ann Arbor: UMI Press, 1981. ii, 170pp.

Analysis of selected piano compositions by Charles Ives using set theory (Forte's Kh-related sets) and computer programs. Nine BASIC programs are employed; code is supplied as Appendix V. Concludes "in spite of numerous appearances of very similar chords throughout, there was no prevailing vertical structure present in all five pieces on which to base the discovery of a continuous musical language (p. 121)." Contains seven appendices and a bibliography.

--- Kolosick, J. Timothy. "A Machine-Independent Data Structure for the Representation of Musical Pitch Relationships: Computer-Generated Musical Examples for CBI." *Journal of Computer-Based Instruction*, 13,1 (Winter 1986): 9-13.

Computer-generated music examples; see main entry no. 128.

63. *Leadsheeter*. Half Moon Bay, Calif.: Passport Designs, n.d. (for Apple II series computers): $149.95.

A software music editor designed to interface with Passport's *MIDI/4* or *MIDI/8* sequencers (item 219). Includes text and music editor, supports dot-matrix printer.

--- Lincoln, Harry B., ed. *The Computer and Music.* Ithaca, N.Y.: Cornell University Press, 1970. 354pp. 0801405505.

Articles on composition; see main entry no. 21.

64. *MacMusic.* Long Beach, Calif.: Utopian Software, 1984. (for Macintosh computers): $89.95.

A music editor with unconventional keyboard and mouse input, no printing capabilities. Offers flexible meters and the ability to produce musical subroutines which can be nested up to 16 levels deep.

Reviews:
Nibble, 6,8 (Aug. 1985): 122-130.
Computer Music Journal, 9,3 (Fall 1985): 52-67.

65. Manning, Peter. "Computers and Music Composition." *Proceedings of the Royal Musical Association,* 107, (1980-1981): 119-131.

A critical assessment of computerized composition with an impressive historical scope. Examines important studios and languages, ending with this cautious assessment of commercially available items: "The outlook for the serious electronic composer is . . . tinged with a growing uncertainty over the suitability of the new technology (p. 130)."

--- Manning, Peter. *Electronic and Computer Music.* Oxford: Clarendon Press, 1985. 291pp. 0193119188. $29.95.

Discussion of early computer composition techniques; see main entry no. 23.

66. Mason, Robert M. *Modern Methods of Music Analysis Using Computers.* Peterborough, N.H.: Schoolhouse Press, 1985. 299pp. 0961566906. $39.50.

A major study of computer applications in music analysis. Divided into two sections, the first part considers introductory topics (computers and notation) while the second develops an extensive methodology for analytic subjects. Includes exercises at the end of each chapter for reinforcing concepts and is oriented toward classroom use on the undergraduate or graduate level. The author emphasizes the usefulness of *Modern Methods* "as foundation material for work on more advanced levels (preface)."

--- Melby, Carol. *Computer Music Compositions of the United States*, 2nd ed. (First International Conference on Computer Music at Illinois). Cambridge, Mass.: MIT Press, 1976. 28pp. 78-305572.

Bibliography of computer compositions; see main entry no. 27.

67. Moomaw, Charles J. "A PL-1 Program for the Harmonic Analysis of Music by the Theories of Paul Hindemith and Howard Hanson." MM Thesis, University of Cincinnati. Ann Arbor: UMI Press, 1973. 2 vols., 135, 143pp.

Not available for review.

68. Morse, Raymond W. "Use of Microcomputer Graphics to Aid in the Analysis of Music." DMA Thesis, University of Oregon. Ann Arbor: UMI Press, 1985. x, 180pp.

Development of the program CAAGS to analyze traditional music statistically and graphically. Parameters include compass, average pitch (sum of all pitches divided by number of pitches), pitch class (conjunct or disjunct), voice count, accidentals count (for any user defined scale), and dissonant intervals count. Provides a model analysis of Debussy's "Yver, vous n'êtes qu'un villain" and concludes there are clear correspondences between traditional analytical techniques and those supplied by CAAGS. Appendices as music coding system, statistics on individual voices, ensemble statistics, CAAGS code for Debussy selection, description of CAAGS programs (no code), score, and bibliography.

69. *Music Composer* (developed by D. Williams). Bellevue, Wash.: Temporal Acuity Products, Inc., ca. 1980. (for Apple II series computers): $150.00.

An early music editor for Apple II series computers. Allows the composition and performance of up to four independent voices using a keyboard code with entry by arrow keys. Supports the construction of timbres and simple editing procedures. DAC board required.

70. *MusicPrinter*, v2.0 (developed by J. Jarrett). Bellevue, Wash.: Temporal Acuity Products, Inc., 1987. (for Apple II Series computers); $149.00.

A music editor for the Apple II series. Entry is by keyboard, mouse, or touch pad; scores may be edited on screen. Offers text, transposition, and block copy capabilities with easy score formatting for traditional ensembles.

71. *MusicType*. Shaherazam (Berkeley, Calif.: Mix Bookshelf), n.d. (for Macintosh computers): $59.95.

An inexpensive music editor with excellent variety of fonts. Especially useful for short examples and tests, input is by QWERTY keyboard.

72. *MusicWorks*. Lowell, Mass.: Hayden Software, 1984. (for Macintosh computers): $79.95.

An inexpensive sequencer, editor, and synthesizer when connected to a Macintosh computer and MIDI instrument interface. Input is by keyboard, mouse, graphics, or MIDI instrument. Supports dot matrix and laser printers.

Reviews:
Personal Computing, 9,5 (May 1985):
    178.
Nibble, 6,8 (Aug. 1985): 122-130.
Macworld, 2,6 (June 1985): 72-79.
Computing Teacher, 12,8 (May 1985):
    38-39.
A+, 3,5 (May 1985): 112-114.
Macworld, 3,12 (Dec. 1986): 109-117.
Computer Music Journal, 9,3 (Fall 1985):
    52-67.

--- Nelson, Randolph. "A Graphics Text Editor for
Music: Structure of the Editor." *Byte,* 5,4 (April
1980): 124-138.

Design characteristics of a music editor;
see main entry no. 267.

73. Pederson, Donald M. "Some Techniques for
Computer-Aided Analysis of Musical Scores." Ph.D.
dissertation, University of Iowa. Ann Arbor: UMI
Press, 1968. 543pp.

Not available for review.

74. *Personal Composer,* v2.0 (developed by J. Miller).
Honaunau, Hawaii: Jim Miller, ca.1983, 1987 (for
IBM PC series computers): $495.00.

One of the most impressive software
packages available for the IBM PC,
Personal Composer is an integrated
sequencer, editor, and voice library.
Offers 32-track recording capability, full
onscreen editing procedures, a timbral
library for Yamaha *DX* or *TX* synthesizers,

and dot-matrix printer support. Requires Roland MIF/IPC interface card (item 223), MIDI hardware interface, and MIDI instrument.

Review:
PC Magazine, 3 (April 3, 1984): 39.

75. *Polywriter*. Half Moon Bay, Calif.: Passport Designs, ca. 1982. (for Apple II series computers): $299.99.

An early music editor for the Apple series computers. Input is by Passport compatible keyboard (sold separately), will support dot-matrix printers. May be interfaced with sequencers by means of the program *Polywriter Utilities* (item 235).

Review:
inCider, 3,3 (March 1985): 85-86.

76. *Professional Composer*, v2.2. Cambridge, Mass.: Mark of the Unicorn, Inc., 1984, 1985, 1987, and 1988. (for Macintosh computers): $495.00.

A most impressive music editor designed for Macintosh computers. Constructed like a menu-driven word processor, *Professional Composer* produces publication quality scores with laser printers. At its best with full scores and parts, polyphonic keyboard scores require a merging technique which slows input down substantially. Interfaces with *Performer* (item 233), a sequencer which transfers MIDI data into *Professional Composer* and allows for the rapid input of scores. Offers

full copying, pasting, transposition, and
editing capabilities.   Latest version
features increased control over note
spacing, use of *Sonata* font (item 83),
slanted beams, improved text editor, and
particularly fine pagination and margin
control.   Although expensive, this editor
makes high-quality scores available to
desktop publishers for the first time.
Excellent manual.

Reviews:
Computer Music Journal, 9,3 (Fall 1985):
    52-67.
A+, 3,10 (Oct. 1985): 132-138.
Macworld, 3,2 (Feb. 1986): 93-99.
Macworld, 3,12 (Dec. 1986): 109-117.

77. Raskin, Jef. "Using the Computer as a Musician's
    Amanuensis, Part 1: Fundamental Problems." *Byte*,
    5,4 (April 1980): 18-28.

    A logical and organized discussion of
    problems associated with constructing
    music editors.

78. Reid, John W. "The Treatment of Dissonance in the
    Works of Guillaume Dufay, A Computer Aided Study."
    Ph.D. dissertation, University of Colorado at Boulder.
    Ann Arbor: UMI Press, 1981. xv, 316pp.

    Classification and analysis of dissonance
    treatment in the works of Dufay
    employing the program Statistical
    Analysis System (=SAS).   Data based upon
    encoding of three masses (selected
    movements), three motets, and twelve
    chansons.   Some 1200 instances of disso-

nance occurrences were encoded using a
variable designation which encompassed
eighteen elements (type of dissonance,
texture, surrounding note values, etc.).
Author concludes Dufay employed
"carefully exercised controls over
dissonances" with a wide variety of
dissonance vocabularies. The incidence of
dissonance within the works analyzed was
not high, corresponding to one occur-
rence every breve, or measure. Bibliography and Appendices.

79. Render, Charles R. "The Development of a Computer
Program to Arrange and Print Traditional Music
Notation." Ed.D. Thesis, University of Illinois at
Urbana-Champaign. Ann Arbor: UMI Press, 1981. vi,
175pp.

Description of the MUSCOR III system for
notating traditional music. Employs
FORTRAN programs with Hewlett-Packard
16-bit mini-computer. Data encoded in
alpha-numeric form, similar (but not
identical) to DARMS. Appendices supplied
as "MUSCOR File List," "MUSCOR File
Descriptions," "Matrix Descriptions,"
"System Generated Messages," and
bibliography.

80. Roads, Curtis, ed. *Composers and the Computer* (The
Computer Music and Digital Audio Series). Los Alto,
Calif.: William Kaufmann, Inc., 1984. xxi, 201pp.
0865760853.

An anthology on computer, linguistic, and
compositional topics with a historically
oriented introduction by Curtis Roads.

Contains interviews with Herbet Brün
(aesthetics and composition), John
Chowning (composition), James Dashow
(history and composition), and George
Lewis (description of AACM, the
Association for the Advancement of
Creative Musicians, and IRCAM). Other
articles include composers discussing
their own works, specifically Charles
Dodge ("In Celebration," with score and
programs), Tod Machover (*Déplacements,
Light*, and *Soft Morning City*) and Curtis
Roads (*nscor*). Concludes with an
excellent article by Xenakis on problems
and solutions in composing computer
music. The latter contains a thought-
provoking appendix on the "correspon-
dance between certain developments in
music and mathematics."

--- Roads, Curtis. "Research in Music and Artificial
Intelligence." *ACM Computing Surveys*, 17,2 (June
1985): 163-190.

Section on artificial intelligence and
composition; see main entry no. 270.

81. Russell, Roberta C. "A Set of Microcomputer
Programs to Aid in the Analysis of Atonal Music."
DMA Thesis, University of Oregon. Ann Arbor: UMI
Press, 1983. ix, 157pp.

Development, description, and application
of two programs written to analyze set
relations. The IDENTIFY program employs
Forte's method of pitch structure and
interval vectors to match the set to the
prime form. The SUBSETS program

considers the order and form of all subsets contained within a larger set. A sample analysis of Webern's *String Quartet*, Op. 5 (fourth movement) describes the effectiveness of the programs. Provides a user's manual and BASIC code in the appendices, bibliography.

82. Smith, Patricia. "Computers Make Music." *Creative Computing*, 9,7 (July 1983): 111-115.

A survey of current microcomputer trends in composition. Includes a brief history of computerized sound production, then emphasizes the activities of the League of Automatic Music Composers based in Oakland, Calif.

83. *Sonata*, v1.6. Mountain View, Calif.: Adobe Systems, Inc., 1987. (for Macintosh computers): $95.00.

A music notation font which employs the *PostScript* language in order to create high quality scores with laser printers. *PostScript* fonts are defined by algorithms and downloaded from the Macintosh system into the volatile memory of the laser printer. Because the font resides in the system as an algorithmic expression, individual symbols may not be altered by the user. However, with the aid of *Fontographer* (Plano, Tex.: Altsys Corp., 1986, $395.00), composite characters may be assembled which satisfy specific needs. *Sonata* font is supported by *Professional Composer* (item 76) and selected other editors.

84. *Songwright+.* Songwright (Berkeley, Calif.: Mix Bookshelf), n.d. (for IBM PC series computers): $74.95.

An inexpensive music editor for IBM computers. Input is by QWERTY keyboard with onscreen editing and transposition features.

85. *The Copyist.* Chestnut Hill, Mass.: Dr. T's Music Software, 1987. (for IBM PC, AT, XT; Atari ST computers): $225.00.

A versatile music editor which supports color graphics and laser printers. Entry is from keyboard, mouse, or MIDI instrument. *Copyist* is compatible with three sequencers: *Texture* (item 244), *Sequencer+* (item 239), and *Master Tracks* (item 212). Offers user definition of ten music characters, an excellent feature for those working with very new or very old music.

86. *The Music Analysis System.* Soft Stuff Computer Software, n.d. (for Apple II and IBM PC series computers): $24.95 and $39.95.

Two software packages for chordal and melodic analysis. Input is by QWERTY keyboard with advanced pattern recognition available in horizontal and vertical planes.

--- *The Music Shop-MIDI.* Half Moon Bay, Calif.: Passport Designs, n.d. (for Commodore series computers): $149.95.

An integrated editor/sequencer package for the Commodore computer; see main entry no. 245.

--- Tjepkema, Sandra L. *A Bibliography of Computer Music: A Reference for Composers*. Iowa City, Iowa: University of Iowa Press, 1981. xvii, 276pp. 0877451109.

Bibliography of compositional sources; see main entry no. 39.

87. Whitney, John. *Digital Harmony: On the Complementarity of Music and Visual Art*. Peterborough, N.H.: Byte Books by McGraw-Hill, 1980. 235pp. 007070015X. $21.95.

An innovative and provocative study considering the relationships between film, graphics, color, and music. Contains a discussion, explanation, and analysis of the author's film/program "Arabesque" (a study in graphics and sound produced by Pascal programs and the filming of a CRT image). Extensive appendices offer selected writings by the author on topics ranging from "color music" and abstract film to self interviews. Bibliography and annotated index.

88. Yavelow, Christopher. "From Keyboard to Score: An Introduction to Music Processing and Evaluations of Six Packages that Put Your Performance on Paper." *Macworld*, 3,12 (Dec. 1986): 109-117.

Excellent introduction into notating and printing music on Macintosh computers

with comparative analysis of seven
software packages: *MusicWorks* (item 72),
ConcertWare (item 53), *Deluxe Music
Construction Set* (item 54), *MegaTrack*
(item 215) *M I D I M a c* (item 2 2 0) ,
Professional Composer (item 76), and
Performer (item 233). A fine first reading
for the musician interested in computerized notation, printing, and publishing.

89. Yavelow, Christopher. "High Score." *MacWorld,* 3,11
(Nov. 1986): 81.

Announcement of Byrd and Stickney's
High Score, a publication quality music
editor/printer for the Macintosh c o m -
puter. As of late 1987, *High Score* was still
in development.

III. Education and Musicianship

90. Allvin, Raynold L. *Basic Musicianship: An Introduction to Music Fundamentals with Computer Assistance*. Belmont, Calif.: Wadsworth Publishing Co., 1985. xi, 180pp. 0534040594. $30.95.

A fundamentals of music text supplemented with 36 software programs. The disk accompanying the text is formatted for Apple II computers and includes exercises as I, sound graph recognition and creation, II, timbral, symbol, and note identification, III, melodic and rhythmic notation, IV, scales, harmonies, a n d chords, V, a minicomposer for simple composition, and VI, a "play along" which aids in learning the soprano recorder. The software produces monophonic sound generation. Students score their computer results on grade sheets provided in the text.

91. Allvin, Raynold L. "Computer-Assisted Music Instruction: A Look at the Potential." Los Gatos, Calif.: IBM Corporation, 1970. 16pp.

An early study of computer assisted instruction produced by IBM Corporation.

Recognizes advantages of the computer as regards individualized instruction, personal graphics, sound, error analysis, and unlimited patience. Develops an instructional system covering four simple areas: ear training, music notation, elementary analysis, and rhythmic discrimination. Designed originally for mainframe devices, the study points toward the need for personal computers for educational and practical reasons.

92. Allvin, Raynold L. "The Development of a Computer-Assisted Music Instruction System to Teach Sight-Singing and Ear Training." DMA Thesis, Stanford University, 1967. Reprint by Mark Larwood Co.: Redwood City, Calif., 1980. 130pp.

Not available for inspection.

93. Arenson, M., and F. Hofstetter. "The GUIDO System and the PLATO Project." *Music Educators Journal*, 69,5 (Jan., 1983): 46-51.

Introduction into the GUIDO (Graded Units for Interactive Dictation Operations) system of CAI instruction. Sample screens provide visual clues about the system along with explanations of teaching theory and new developments. Bibliography.

94. Arenson, Michael. "The Effect of a Competency-Based Computer Program on the Learning of Fundamental Skills in a Music Theory Course for Non-Majors." *Journal of Computer-Based Instruction*, 9,2 (Autumn 1982): 55-58.

Not available for review.

95. *Arnold* (developed by J. Timothy Kolosick).
Bellevue, Wash.: Temporal Acuity Products, Inc., ca.
1980. (for Apple II series computers): $150.00.

A well constructed melodic dictation and
memory program. Suitable for fourth
graders to adults, the program plays
increasingly difficult melodies which are
notated by the user through solfeggio o r
scale degree numbers. Requires DAC
board.

96. Bales, W. Kenton. "Computer-Based Instruction and
Music Technology in Education." *Journal of
Computer-Based Instruction*, 13,1 (Winter 1986): 2-5.

Broad based discussion of the development
and impact of technology on the musical
world. Includes specific CBI considerations of musicianship, word processing,
database, and linguistic parameters.

97. Bamberger, Jeanne. "Logo Music." *Byte*, 7,8 (Aug.
1982): 325-328.

Brief description of the Logo musical language.

98. Canelos, Murphy, Blombach, and Heck. "Evaluation
of Three Types of Instructional Strategy for
Learner Acquisition of Intervals." *Journal of
Research in Music Education*, 28 (1980): 243-249.

Not available for inspection.

99. *Catch the Key* (developed by J. Moore). Bellevue, Wash.: Temporal Acuity Products, Inc., n.d. (for Apple II series computers): $50.00.

> A CAD software program providing exercise in key recognition. Covers major and minor keys on four clefs. DAC board required.

100. *Chord Mania* (developed by D. Williams, J. Schulze, and D. Shrader). Bellevue, Wash.: Temporal Acuity Products, Inc., ca. 1980. (for Apple II series computers): $125.00.

> CAD instruction in harmonic dictation wherein one or two players try to "beat the clock" and guess the correct quality of the chord (major, minor, diminished, etc.). Allows some instructor control over the ordering of examples. Requires DAC board.

101. De Laine, Thomas H. "The Status of Music Education in the Public Schools of Maryland, 1983-84." DMA Thesis, The Catholic University. Ann Arbor: UMI Press, 1986. 249pp.

> Not available for review.

102. *Diatonic Chords* (developed by J. McCarthy and D. Para). Bellevue, Wash.: Temporal Acuity Products, Inc., ca. 1980. (for Apple II series computers): $150.00.

> A CAI software program for instruction in traditional four-part writing. The student hears a passage, then identifies

the bass notes, soprano notes, and chord
function. Examples are locked in order.
Requires DAC board.

103. *Doremi* (developed by B. Benward and D. Williams).
Bellevue, Wash.: Temporal Acuity Products Inc.,
ca. 1980. (for Apple II series computers): $75.00.

Ear training program which provides
CAD instruction in major mode scale
degrees. Plays random sequence of up
to four notes (no score on screen);
student supplies solfeggi response.
Requires DAC board.

104. Duncan, Danny J. "Practices and Standards in the
Teaching of Woodwind Technique Classes in the
Music Education Curriculum in Selected Colleges
and Universities in the United States." DME Thesis,
Indiana University. Ann Arbor: UMI Press, 1978.
155pp.

Not Available for inspection.

---- Eddins, John M. "A Brief History of Computer-
Assisted Instruction in Music." *College Music
Symposium*, 21,2 (Fall 1981): 7-14.

See main entry no. 12.

105. Edwards, John S. "A Model Computer Assisted
Information Retrieval System in Music
Education." Ed.D. dissertation, University of
Georgia. Ann Arbor: UMI Press, 1969. 197pp.

Development of computerized systems for indexing, storing, and retrieving music education data. Appendices: thesaurus building, types of indexing, data file, and bibliography.

106. Foltz, R., and D. Gross. "Integration of CAI into a Music Program." *Journal of Computer-Based Instruction*, 6,3 (1980): 72-76.

Not available for review.

107. Franklin, James L. "What's a Computer Doing in My Music Room?" *Music Educators Journal*, 69,5 (Jan. 1983): 29-32.

Call for computer literacy and explanation of CAI principles. Discusses problems associated with computerized instruction including inadequate instructional programs, software incompatibility, lack of instrumental programs, and the difficulty of assessing effectiveness in CAI methodology.

108. Glass, Jacqualine S. "The Effects of a Microcomputer-Assisted Tuning Program on Junior High School Students' Pitch Discrimination and Pitch-Matching Abilities." Ph.D. dissertation, University of Miami. Ann Arbor: UMI Press, 1986. 102pp.

Not available for review.

109. Green, Gussie L. "Instructional Use of

Microcomputers in Indiana Public High Schools."
Ed.D. dissertation, Ball State University. Ann
Arbor: UMI Press, 1983. 255pp.

Not available for review.

110. Greenfield, D., and P. Codding. "Competency-Based
Vs. Linear Computer Instruction of Music
Fundamentals." *Journal of Computer-Based
Instruction*, 12,4 (Autumn 1985): 108-110.

A carefully constructed study of the
efficacy of CAI employing 97 university
students (non-music majors). Differ-
entiates between linear-programmed
computer lessons and competency-based
ones; concludes that "instructional
strategy, not technology, influences
learning (p. 110)." A comparison of
teaching strategies indicates the group
using competency-based computer lessons scored significantly higher in
testing situations than three other
groups. Bibliography.

111. Grijalva, Francisco J. "Factors Influencing
Computer Use by Music Educators in California
Independent Elementary and Secondary Schools."
Ed.D. dissertation, University of San Francisco.
Ann Arbor: UMI Press, 1986. 190pp.

Not available for inspection.

112. Gross, D., and R. Foltz. "Ideas on Implementation
and Evaluation of a Music CAI Project." *College
Music Symposium*, 21,2 (Fall 1981): 22-26.

Testing program designed to evaluate the effectiveness of CAI instruction. Authors constructed MUSFUND, a series of twenty drills on theory topics and applied the programs to music fundamentals courses in Nebraska and Minnesota. Concludes: I, the computer system must be affordable, II, students should improve as a result of CAI, III, lessons must be easy to use, IV, CAI should not be so uninteresting that students stop using it, V, evaluation should be a continuing process before and after CAI use, and VI, attitude and achievement should be measured separately.

113. Grushcow, B. "Computers in the Private Studio." *Music Educators Journal*, 71,5 (Jan. 1985): 25-29.

Practical guidelines for the selection of hardware and software of use to studio teachers. Provides information on tax deductions and a sample list of software. Bibliography.

114. *Harmonious Dictator* (developed by J. Kolosick and D. Williams). Bellevue, Wash.: Temporal Acuity Products, Inc., ca. 1980. (for Apple II series computers): $150.00.

One of the more flexible and intriguing harmonic dictation programs to appear in the early 1980s. The student is presented with a series of chords heard blind. He or she then sees a score on the screen along with the correct key and first chord. Input for the next chord's

function and inversion is made by left
and right keyboard arrows. A chal-
lenging program with subtleties such as
automatic selection of skill level. DAC
board required.

115. *Harmony Drills: Set I* (developed by B. Benward
and J. Kolosick), Bellevue, Wash.: Temporal Acuity
Products, Inc., ca. 1980. (for Apple II series
computers): $90.00.

A CAD software instruction program
which plays simple, diatonic chord
progressions. Students select from five
levels of difficulty and enter their
answer with one of three keys. Serves
as a supplement to Benward's cassette
series, *Ear Training, A Technique for
Listening* (2nd ed., Dubuque, Iowa: W.C.
Brown Co., 1983; see also *Music in
Theory and Practice: Volumes I and II*,
3rd edition, item 140). DAC board
required.

116. Hofstetter, Fred T. "Applications of the GUIDO
System to Aural Skills Research, 1975-80." *College
Music Symposium*, 21,2 (Fall 1981): 46-53.

A perceptive study considering one
major aspect of CAI design: how best to
organize small modules of learning and
their content. Offers four research
results: I, recognition of perceptual
patterns, II, discovery of data dispelling
commonly held beliefs, III, controlled
evaluation of instructional methods, and
IV, effects of difficulty upon learning
style.

117. Hofstetter, Fred T. "Computer-Based Recognition of Perceptual Patterns in Chord Quality Dictation Exercises." *Journal of Research in Music Education*, 28 (Summer 1980): 83-91.

Not available for review.

118. Hofstetter, Fred T. "Evaluation of a Competency-Based Approach to Teaching Aural Interval Identification." *Journal of Research in Music Education*, 27 (Winter 1979): 201-213.

Not available for inspection.

119. Hofstetter, Fred T. "GUIDO: An Interactive Computer-Based System for Improvement of Instruction and Research in Ear-Training." *Journal of Computer-Based Instruction*, 3 (May 1975): 100-106.

Not available for review.

120. Hofstetter, Fred T. "Instructional Design and Curricular Impact of Computer-Based Music Education." *Educational Technology*, 18 (April 1978): 50-53.

Not available for review.

121. Hofstetter, Fred T. "Microelectronics and Music Education." *Music Educators Journal*, (April 1979): 38-45.

Not available for review.

122. Holland, Penny. *Looking at Computer Sounds and Music* (An Easy-Read Computer Activity Book). New York: Franklin Watts, 1986. 32pp. 0531100979.

> Children's introduction to computers and fundamentals of music (the latter as basic acoustical concepts). Includes activities keyed to text, games, simple programs, and physical activities.

123. *Interval Mania* (developed by D. Williams, J. Schulze, and D. Shrader). Bellevue, Wash.: Temporal Acuity Products, Inc., ca. 1980. (for Apple II series computers): $150.00.

> Similar in format to *Chord Mania* (item 100), this CAD software program offers one or two players a chance to select the correct interval and "beat the clock." *Interval Mania* keeps score and requires a DAC board.

124. *Jazz Dictator* (developed by D. Williams, J. Kolosick, and D. Haerle). Bellevue, Wash.: Temporal Acuity Products, Inc., ca. 1980. (for Apple II series computers): $150.00.

> The chromatic version of *Harmonious Dictator* (item 114). *Jazz Dictator* supplies examples such as chromatic progressions, borrowed chords, and secondary dominants; it will automatically adjust the level of skill. Requires DAC board.

125. *Key Signature Drills* (developed by G. Makas).

Bellevue, Wash.: Temporal Acuity Products, Inc., n.d. (for Apple II series computers): $60.00.

A CAD software program which provides exercises for key and scale identification. Includes aural and visual methods for recognizing key, tonic, and scale mode together with a game option. DAC board required.

126. Killam, Baczewski, Corbet, Dworak, et al. "Research Applications in Music CAI." *College Music Symposium*, 21,2 (Fall 1981): 37-44.

Thoughtful statement of research problems associated with developing CAI systems. Includes suggestions in four main areas: I, research in modeling the student, II, research in curriculum design, III, research in hardware and software, and IV, research in data saving and analysis. Bibliography.

127. Kirshbaum, Thomas K. "Using a Touch Tablet as an Effective, Low-Cost Input Device in a Melodic Dictation Game." *Journal of Computer-Based Instruction*, 13,1 (Winter 1986): 14-16.

Employment of a touch pad for entering keyboard symbols. Kirshbaum's testing method interfaces the pad with *Tunemaster*, a melodic dictation program. Early tests report advantages such as ease of use and heuristic learning supported by immediate feedback. Disadvantages resulted from the uncomfortable feel of the tablet and the potential loss of notational skills.

128. Kolosick, J. Timothy. "A Machine-Independent Data Structure for the Representation of Musical Pitch Relationships: Computer-Generated Musical Examples for CBI." *Journal of Computer-Based Instruction*, 13,1 (Winter 1986): 9-13.

> Intriguing development of an algorithm which creates musical examples for CBI purposes. Assigns patterns and discrete values to multiple arrays using offset relationships.

129. Kuyper, Jon Q. "A Computer-Assisted Instruction System in Music Theory and Fundamentals." Ph.D. dissertation, University of Iowa. Ann Arbor: UMI Press, 1981. 262pp.

> Not available for inspection.

130. Lemons, Robert M. "The Development and Trial of Microcomputer-Assisted Techniques to Supplement Traditional Training in Musical Sightreading." DMA Thesis, University of Colorado. Ann Arbor: UMI Press, 1984. x, 125pp.

> Construction of twenty programs de-signed to improve sightreading and test the effectiveness of CAI instruction. Programs are based on tachistoscopic training techniques. Concludes "the supplementary sightreading materials had a significant positive effect on students who used them during the experiment (p. 57)." Nine appendices such as test descriptions, raw data and tables, general program descriptions (no code), lesson logs, and bibliography.

131. *MacVoice* (developed by M. Thomas and P. Monta). Santa Barbara, Calif.: Kinko's Academic Courseware Exchange, 1985. (for Macintosh computers): approx. $30.00.

> Inexpensive program which teaches rules of part writing. Student selects bass note, then constructs three more voices by mouse input. MacVoice will automatically assess part writing mistakes and provide a list of error and location statements (e.g., "parallel fifths in bass and alto between chords 1 and 2"). The program automatically provides figured bass and accepts up to 50 chords in a single sequence. Any major or minor key can be selected and examples can be saved, played back, and printed (supports dot-matrix "screen dumps" only).

132. *Magic Musical Balloon Game* (developed by S. Monsour and C. Knox). Bellevue, Wash.: Temporal Acuity Products, Inc., n.d. (for Apple II series computers): $25.00.

> A melodic CAI software program for teaching young students. Relates melodic direction to the movement of a balloon and requests the child to duplicate patterns. Suitable for early elementary instruction.

133. Malone, Thomas W. "What Makes Things Fun to Learn? A Study of Intrinsically Motivating Computer Games." Ph.D. dissertation, Stanford University. Ann Arbor: UMI Press, 1980. 93pp.

Not available for inspection.

134. Meckley, William A. "The Development of Individualized Music Learning Sequences for Non-Handicapped, Handicapped and Gifted Learners Using the LOGO Music Version Computer Language." Ph.D. dissertation, University of Rochester. Ann Arbor: UMI Press, 1984.

> The development of teaching and learning strategies using LOGO and its philosophy of developed microworlds. Considers advantages and disadvantages of LOGO instruction for three classes of students. Apple II hardware, BASIC programs, and ALF model *MCI Musicard* employed.

135. *Melodious Dictator* (developed by D. Williams and D. Shrader). Bellevue, Wash.: Temporal Acuity Products, Inc., ca. 1980. (for Apple II series computers): $150.00.

> An early and influential melodic trainer designed for the Apple computer. The student hears a melody played blind, then sees a score representation onscreen with the correct key and first note. Successive notes are entered by arrow keys positioned on a keyboard which is found directly below the staff. Automatically adjusts skill level and supplies test results at the end of the program.

136. *Melody Race* (developed by J., R., and A. Matheny)

Bellevue, Wash.: Temporal Acuity Products, Inc.,
n.d. (for Commodore series computers): $40.00.

A CAD software program for solfege
recognition. Organized as a "beat-the
clock" game, the student selects letters,
solfege syllables, or numbers in order to
label a given melody.

137. *Micro Brass Series* (available for trumpet, horn,
baritone, and tuba; developed by W. Higgins and D.
Williams). Bellevue, Wash.: Temporal Acuity
Products, Inc., n.d. (for Apple II series
computers): $70.00 each; set $295.00.

A performance oriented CAI software
package that teaches the fingering of
brass instruments. Requires a micro-
valve simulator for input ($70.00) and
DAC board.

138. Millar, Jana K. "The Aural Perception of Pitch-
Class Set Relations: A Computer-Assisted
Investigation." Ph.D. dissertation, North Texas
State University. Ann Arbor: UMI Press, 1984.
237pp.

Not available for review.

139. *Mode Drills* (developed by G. Makas). Bellevue,
Wash.: Temporal Acuity Products, Inc., ca. 1980.
(for Apple II series computers): $70.00.

Excellent CAD software tutor for mode
recognition. The student selects from
seven modes which may be constructed
on any chromatic tonic. Provides test

results and self-paced skill levels. DAC
board required.

140. *Music in Theory and Practice*, Volumes I and II,
3rd edition (developed by B. Benward, B. Moore,
and D. Williams). Bellevue, Wash.: Temporal Acuity
Products, Inc., ca. 1980. (for Apple II series
computers): $350.00 and $275.00.

> Set of CAD software programs which
> accompany Benward's text *Music in
> Theory and Practice*. Some fourteen
> disks provide personalized tutorials for
> all non-creative assignments in the text.
> DAC board required.

141. *Musicland*. FreeLance MusicWorks, 1984. (for
Apple II series computers): $99.95.

> A well designed software package which
> introduces principles of music composi-
> tion to young students. Four musical
> "playgrounds" change shapes into
> melodies, colors into timbres, blocks
> into forms, and allows users to "draw"
> envelopes. Requires purchase of sound
> board manufactured by the Classic
> Organ Company.

> Review:
> *Computing Teacher*, 12,8 (May 1985):
> 34-36.

142. *Name It: Kids' Classics* (developed by B. Benward
and D. Williams). Bellevue, Wash.: Temporal Acuity
Products, Inc., ca. 1980. (for Apple II series
computers): $40.00.

A "name that tune" type of program
which teaches scale recognition and
melodic remembrance. Twenty-four
different melodies are available for
recognition; highest points are awarded
if you guess the name in the fewest
notes. Requires DAC board.

143. Parrish, James W. "Computer Research as a Course
of Study in Music Education: Development of an
Exemplary Sequence of Teacher-Guided and Self-
Instructional Learning Modules for College Music
Majors." Ph.D. dissertation, Florida State
University. Ann Arbor: UMI Press, 1977. vii,
400pp. 78-15475.

Development of materials for a college
course on computer applications in
music. Divides into three general areas:
introduction to computers, readings, and
interaction with software and hardware.
Bibliography.

---- Peters, G., and J. Eddins. "Applications of
Computers to Music Pedagogy, Analysis, and
Research: A Selected Bibliography." *Journal of
Computer-Based Instruction*, 5,1-2 (Aug. and Nov.
1978): 41-44.

Pedagogical bibliography; see main entry, no. 32.

144. Peters, G. David. "Hardware Development for
Computer-Based Instruction." *College Music
Symposium*, 21,2 (Fall 1981): 15-21.

Introduction to hardware topics for CBI
use and specific discussion of D/A
converters.

145. *Pick the Pitch* (developed by B. Moore). Bellevue,
Wash.: Temporal Acuity Products, Inc., n.d. (for
Apple II series computers): $50.00.

A pitch recognition CAD software
program. DAC board required.

146. *Pitch Drills With Accidentals* (developed by G.
Makas). Bellevue, Wash.: Temporal Acuity
Products, Inc. ca. 1980. (for Apple II series
computers): $50.00.

A pitch recognition CAD software
package. Produces all chromatic pitches
on two clefs; offers transposition capabilities. DAC board required.

147. *Pitch Drills Without Accidentals* (developed by G.
Makas). Bellevue, Wash.: Temporal Acuity
Products, Inc., ca. 1980. (for Apple II series
computers): $50.00.

A CAD software program which teaches
pitch recognition. Supplies diatonic
exercises on two clefs. DAC board
required.

148. *Pitch Duel* (developed by J., R., and A. Matheny).
Bellevue, Wash.: Temporal Acuity Products, Inc.,
n.d. (for Commodore series computers): $40.00.

A CAD software program for interval
and chord recognition. The student
hears the interval or chord then
replicates unknown pitches on a staff
using arrow keys. Forty skill levels
covering chromatic intervals and most
chords.

149. *Pitch-u-lation* (developed by J., R., and A.
Matheny). Bellevue, Wash.: Temporal Acuity
Products, Inc., n.d. (for Commodore series
computers): $40.00.

A CAD software program for developing
pitch memory. User input is by light
pen or arrow keys. *Pitch-u-lation* offers
six skill levels.

150. Prevel, M., and F. Sallis. "Real-Time Generation of
Harmonic Progression in the Context of
Microcomputer-Based Ear Training." *Journal of
Computer-Based Instruction*, 13,1 (Winter 1986): 6-
8.

Construction of an algorithm which
produces real-time harmonic progressions. Employs standard rules of four-
part writing in a computerized context
which offers considerable choice by the
user. Progressions are constructed from
the final cadence backwards.

151. *Rhythm Drills* (developed by G. Makas). Bellevue,
Wash.: Temporal Acuity Products, Inc., ca. 1980.
(for Apple II series computers): $75.00.

A CAI software program for instruction
in rhythmic patterns. Employs traditional notation and selection of
individual note values; examples are
supplied with accompanying melodic
shapes. Requires DAC board.

152. *Rhythm Machine* (developed by D. Otterson).
Bellevue, Wash.: Temporal Acuity Products, Inc.,
n.d. (for Apple II series computers): $60.00.

A rhythmic CAI software program. The
program plays a short melody and four
rhythmic choices are projected on the
screen. The student selects the correct
answer as quickly as possible in order to
improve his or her score. DAC board
required.

153. *Rhythm Write* (developed by I. Polster). Bellevue,
Wash.: Temporal Acuity Products, Inc., n.d. (for
Apple II series computers): $90.00.

A rhythmic CAI software program.
Follows traditional ear training practice; the student hears a pattern and
repeats the rhythmic sequences. Ten
skill levels are available and the
program records the student's progress.
DAC board required.

154. *Rhythmaticity* (developed by J., R., and A.
Matheny). Bellevue, Wash.: Temporal Acuity
Products, Inc., n.d. (for Commodore series
computers): $75.00.

A CAD software program for rhythmic dictation. The user taps a previously heard sequence on the keyboard for practice; contains 30 skill levels.

155. *Rhythmic Dictator* (developed by D. Shrader and D. Williams). Bellevue, Wash.: Temporal Acuity Products, Inc., ca. 1981. (for Apple II series computers): $125.00.

Rhythm and memory software for CAI instruction. The user hears a rhythmic pattern, in varying tempos and meters, and selects the correct pattern for each measure. Automatically adjusts skill level. DAC board required.

156. Rumery, Kenneth R. "Bringing Your Classroom Online." *Music Educators Journal*, 71,5 (Jan. 1985): 20-24.

General description of the advantages and capabilities of microcomputers for classroom purposes. Provides a non-technical introduction suitable for computer literacy courses and concludes with a plea for better music languages and more integrated software.

157. Rumery, Kenneth R. "Computer Applications in Music Education." *T.H.E. Journal*, 14,2 (Sept. 1986): 97-99.

Survey results describing the use of microcomputers in postsecondary schools. One hundred respondents tell of the broad based use of microcomputers for research, administrative, and musical purposes. Defines typical installations (with emphasis on Apple computers), offers suggestions for improvement, and relates views toward contemporary, computerized methods.

158. Sanders, William H. "The Effect of Computer-Based Instructional Materials in a Program for Visual Diagnostic Skills Training of Instrumental Music Education Students." Ph.D. dissertation, University of Illinos at Champaign-Urbana. Ann Arbor: UMI Press, 1980. 129pp.

Not available for review.

159. Schnebly, B. Julia. "Effects of Two Music Labeling Systems on Cognitive Processing: A Comparison of MOD 12 and Diatonic Terminology." Ph.D. dissertation, University of Washington. Ann Arbor: UMI Press, 1984. 199pp.

Not available for review.

160. Schooley, John H. "Learning and Teaching through Technology at Home and in School; Computers Open the Door to New Ways of Mastering Music." *High Fidelity*, 34 (Feb. 1984): in *Musical America* insert, pp. 14ff.

Not available for review.

161. Schwaegler, David G. "A Computer-Based Trainer for Music Conducting: The Effects of Four Feedback Modes." Ph.D. dissertation, University of Iowa. Ann Arbor: UMI Press, 1984. vii, 148pp.

Interactive design of a microcomputer based conducting tool which provides Immediate Feedback (=IF) for accuracy of the pattern, steadiness of the beat, and comparison to an ideal model. Termed a Music Conducting Trainer (=MCT), programs were executed on Apple hardware with newly constructed software. Conclusions center on the nature of continuous versus discontinuous feedback in the training mode and suggest that extreme accuracy of beat is neither possible nor desirable.

162. *Sebastian II* (developed by B. Moore). Bellevue, Wash.: Temporal Acuity Products, Inc., n.d. (for Apple II series computers): $125.00.

A melodic CAI software program. The user sees a melody on the screen while the computer plays it with one wrong note (randomly selected). Errors can be of note or pitch. *Sebastian* keeps the student's score on disk. DAC board required.

163. Sherborn, James W. "Chips and Diodes of Microcomputers." *Music Educators Journal*, 69,5 (Jan. 1983): 32-38.

A practical consideration of the nature and advantages of microcomputers. Concludes the wise music teacher will consider three factors when choosing a microcomputer system: objectives and needs, software, and affordable hardware. Bibliography.

164. Shrader, David L. "Microcomputer-Based Teaching: Computer-Assisted Instruction of Music Comes of Age." *College Music Symposium*, 21,2 (Fall 1981): 27-36.

> Excellent assessment of the role of computers in education and the impact of microcomputer technology and affordability on the academic world (as of 1981). Provides five rules for good software design and concludes "The microcomputer revolution in music instruction has already occurred and it is only now a matter of time before it permeates all levels of instruction (p. 36)."

165. *Sir William Wrong Note* (developed by J. Kolosick). Bellevue, Wash.: Temporal Acuity Products, Inc., ca. 1980. (for Apple II series computers): $150.00.

> A harmonic CAI software program. Plays a four voice chord with one note wrong and requests the user to identify that note and its correct placement. Suitable for sophisticated use by conductors and educators. DAC board required.

166. Tashjian, Thomas A. "Contingent Sensory Stimulation and Productive Vocal Responding in Profoundly Retarded Multiply-Handicapped Children." Ph.D. dissertation, University of Rhode Island. Ann Arbor: UMI Press, 1981. 111pp.

> Not available for review.

167. Taylor, Jack A. "Computers as Music Teachers."
Music Educators Journal, 69,5 (Jan. 1983): 43-45.

> Theoretical account of a CBI system
> (=computer-based instruction) which
> emphasizes video disk and computer
> technology.

168. Taylor, Jack A. "The MEDICI Melodic Dictation
Computer Program: Its Design, Management, and
Effectiveness as Compared to Classroom Melodic
Notation." *Journal of Computer-Based Instruction*,
9,2 (Autumn 1982): 64-73.

> Not available for review.

169. *The GUIDO Ear-Training System* (developed by F.
Hofstetter). Delaware, Md.: University of Delaware,
1986. (for IBM PC series, and Macintosh
computers):   pricing   unavailable.

> An exceptionally well designed and
> inclusive software system for
> instruction in musicianship.   Based on
> effective educational principles *GUIDO*
> offers CAI in all major theoretical areas
> (intervals, melodies, chords, harmony,
> and rhythm) with individual lessons
> adjustable by the instructor.   Students
> enjoy full record keeping capabilities
> on magnetic disk.

170. *The Music Detective* (developed by J., R., and A.
Matheny). Bellevue, Wash.: Temporal Acuity
Products, Inc., n.d. (for Commodore series
computers): $60.00.

A CAD software program for detecting pitch and rhythmic errors. The student locates a pitch or rhythm error in the context of a supplied melody. *The Music Detective* produces ten skill levels.

171. *Theory Sampler* (developed by D. Bowers and D. Williams). Bellevue, Wash.: Temporal Acuity Products, Inc., n.d. (for Apple II series computers): $125.00.

CAI software instruction in five areas: scale and mode recognition, triad and 7th-chord recognition, scale and mode construction, triad construction, and 7th-chord construction.

172. *Toney Listens to Music* (by D. Williams and D. Fox). Bellevue, Wash.: Temporal Acuity Products, Inc., n.d. (for Apple II series computers): $90.00.

A comprehensive CAI software program for the young. The child learns to differentiate between identical and different tunes, intervals, tempos, timbres, and rhythms. DAC board required.

173. Turk. "Development of the Music Listening Strategy--TEMPO: Computer Assisted Instruction in Music Listening." Ph.D. dissertation, University of Kansas. Ann Arbor: UMI Press, 1983. ix, 193pp.

A series of tempo discrimination programs designed to check the efficacy of computer-assisted instruction. Employs test and control groups in a three stage format: pretest, instruction, and

posttest.   Results indicate effective
learning occurred in eleven- to
fourteen-year-olds.

---- Upitis, Rena. "Milestones in Computer Music
Instruction." *Music Educators Journal*, 69,5 (Jan.
1983): 40-42.

> Historical summary of CAI from 1970 to
> 1983; see main entry no. 40.

174. Wagganer, John W. "A Comparison of Attitudes
Toward Science Held by Teachers, Principals, and
Parents in the State of Missouri." Ed.D.
dissertation, University of Missouri. Ann Arbor:
UMI Press, 1984. 169pp.

> Not available for review.

175. Wallace, Robert L. "Your Sort of Computer
Program!" *Music Educators Journal*, 71,5 (Jan.
1985): 33-36.

> BASIC program which creates a database
> for handling contest information.

---- Wittlich, Schaffer, and Babb. *Microcomputers and
Music*. Englewood Cliffs, N.J.: Prentice-Hall, 1986.
xiii, 321pp. 0135805155.

> Programming instructions for CAI pro-
> grams; see main entry no. 275.

---- Wolfe, George. "Creative Computers--Do They

'Think'?" *Music Educators Journal*, 69,5 (Jan. 1983): 59-62.

Considers feasibility of teaching creativity; see main entry no. 43.

176. Wood, R., and P. Clements. "Systematic Evaluation Strategies for Computer-Based Music Instruction Systems." *Journal of Computer-Based Instruction*, 13,1 (Winter 1986): 17-24.

Description of a CAI system employing variable instructor control over the computer generation of examples. Weighs the efficacy of the teaching strategy against the performance of the student. The author claims the system produces "concrete, quantitative information with which to judge the efficiency and effectiveness of program operation (p. 24)." A worthy contribution, one that addresses the need for flexible instruction and methodology in microcomputer usage.

177. Yavelow, Christopher. "Berklee School of Music." *Macworld*, 4,6 (June 1987): 109-111.

Description of the education, hardware, and networking system employed by the Music Synthesis Program at Berklee (Boston, Mass.).

178. Zuk, Dorothy A. "The Effects of Microcomputers on
Children's Attention to Reading Tasks." Ph.D.
dissertation, University of Kentucky. Ann Arbor:
UMI Press, 1985. 132pp.

Not available for review.

IV. Interfaces:
Sequencers, MIDI, Related
Hardware and Design

179. *Amiga MIDI Interface.* Palo Alto, Calif.: Mimetics, n.d. (for Amiga Computers): $49.00.

> A MIDI hardware interface for Amiga computers; requires MIDI instrument and sequencer.

180. Anderson, J., and R. Swirsky. "Outpost: Atari: The State of Atari and a Musical Instrument to Make." *Creative Computing*, 11,3 (March 1985): 152-153.

> Clever program and hardware addition which turns an Atari computer into a functioning Theremin. Simple circuitry could be adapted easily to other computers.

181. Anderton, Craig. *MIDI for Musicians.* New York: Amsco Publications, 1986. xiii, 105pp. 0825610508. $14.95.

> A MIDI manual oriented toward the

practicing musician. Clear, well organized text covers application topics and
includes references to more popular
hardware items. A useful "sequencer
comparison checklist" offers a
systematic approach for selecting the
best sequencer for your needs.
Appendices: MIDI 1.0 specifications,
troubleshooting guide, and list of MIDI
organizations.

182. *Apple Series MIDI Interface with Drum Sync.* Half
Moon Bay, Calif.: Passport Designs, n.d. (for Apple
II series computers): $129.95.

A MIDI hardware interface for Apple
computers; requires MIDI instrument
and sequencer. Available with Tape
Sync for $70.00 additional. Owners of
Apple IIc models should purchase *Apple
IIc MIDI Pro Interface.*

183. Baker, Robert W. "Uncovering the C-64's CIA: New
Adapter Chip Features I-O Port, Timers and More."
Microcomputing, 7,8 (Aug. 1983): 18-22.

Technical description of the Commodore
64 CIA (=Complex Interface Adapter)
including hardware cartridge *Music
Machine.*

184. "Buyer's Guide to Music Hardware and Software
(1986); Regardless of Musical Talent, Your Family
Can Make Beautiful Music." *Family Computing*, 4,8
(Aug. 1986): 36-40.

Survey of hardware and software items available for popular computers (Apple, Macintosh, Atari, Coleco Adam, Commodore, IBM, and Tandy). Comparative tables judge performance characteristics and ease of use and provide prices and manufacturers' addresses.

185. Carr, Joseph J. *Designing Microprocessor-Based Instrumentation*. Reston, Va.: Prentice-Hall, 1982. ix, 323pp. 0835912701.

An explanation of the technical and engineering side of computers. Based on two microprocessors, the Zilog Z80 and MOS 6502.

186. Carr, Joseph J. *Digital Interfacing with an Analog World*, 2nd ed. Blue Ridge Summit, Pa.: TAB Books, Inc., 1978, 1987. xiii, 464pp. 0830609504. $25.95.

Technical, design, and engineering coverage of digital devices and sample analog converters. Chapters on "Elements of computer interfacing" (#22, pp. 414-427) and "Single-board and small computers (#23, pp. 428-443) added for the second edition.

187. Carr, Joseph J. *Elements of Microcomputer Interfacing*. Reston, Va.: Prentice-Hall, 1984. x, 387pp. 0835917053h, 0835917045p.

Excellent introduction into microcomputer design and related considerations of input and output. Includes two major chapters on "Interfacing with the

real world: the analog subsystem" (#11,
pp. 238-309) and "Data conversion:
Techniques and interfacing" (#12, pp.
310-349). Useful appendix offers "fast
Fourier transform for Apple II users"
(pp. 366-381), an assembly language
program which allows rapid determina-
tion of frequency components.

188. Carr, Joseph J. *Microcomputer Interfacing
Handbook: A/D & D/A.* Blue Ridge Summit, Pa.: TAB
Books, Inc., 1980. 350pp. 0830697047. $14.95.

Design and implementation of D/A and
A/D conversion. Supported by liberal
use of schematics and diagrams, the
work describes both conversion principles and microcomputer interfacing.

189. Casabona, H., and D. Frederick. *Using MIDI* (A
Keyboard Magazine Book). Sherman Oaks, Calif.:
Alfred Publishing Co. Inc., 1987. iv, 123pp.
0882843540. $12.95.

A practical guide to MIDI applications
designed to proceed from simple to
complex issues. Outlines introductory
topics (performance controls, channels,
and modes), applications (sequencers,
drum machines, timing, keyboards and
effects), and advanced topics (timecodes,
sync interface, video syncing). Appendices: reading MIDI implementation
charts, MIDI 1.0 specifications, and a list
of MIDI manufacturers.

---- Ciarcia, Steve. "Sound Off." *Byte,* 4,7 (July 1979):

34-51.

Assembly language programs necessary for interfacing sound chips to computers; see main entry no. 283.

190. *Commodore 64/128 MIDI Interface.* Canoga Park, Calif.: Sonus, n.d. (for Commodore series computers): $75.00.

A MIDI hardware interface for Commodore series computers; requires sequencer software.

191. *Commodore Series MIDI Interface with Drum Sync.* Half Moon Bay, Calif.: Passport Designs, n.d. (for Commodore series computers): $129.95.

A MIDI hardware interface for Commodore 64 and 128 computers. Requires MIDI instrument and sequencer software. A version is available with tape sync for an additional $70.00.

192. Cowart, R., and S. Cummings. "A New Musical Revolution: What Is MIDI, and How Does Your Apple II Fit In?" *A+*, 4,2 (Feb. 1986): 27-32.

Practical discussion of MIDI uses for Apple II computers. Topics include sequencers, transcribing, programming synthesizers, hardware, cost, and availability.

193. De Furia, S., and J. Scacciaferro. *The Midi Book:*

Using Midi and Related Interfaces. Rutherford,
N.J.: Third Earth Productions, Inc., 1986. 95pp.
0881885142. $14.95.

A simple and effective introduction into
the world of MIDI interfaces designed
for the non-technical reader. Numerous diagrams and practical analogies
explain synthesizer to synthesizer and
synthesizer to computer interfacing
with clarity and ease. An excellent
volume for the electronic keyboardist or
for introductory courses in synthesizer
and computer applications.

194. De Furia, S., and J. Scacciaferro. *The Midi Resource
Book.* Pompton Lakes, N.J.: Third Earth Publishing
Inc., 1987. 149pp. 0881885878. $17.95.

First in a series of three books defining
MIDI applications. Provides detailed
specifications for MIDI interface, considers the newest implementations and
extensions of the standard, and
describes exclusive formats for specific
manufacturers. Valuable appendices
include MIDI organizations, manu-
facturer's addresses, online resources,
educational sources, books and publications, and technical support.

195. De Furia, S., and J. Scacciaferro. *The Midi
Implementation Book.* Pompton Lakes, N.J.: Third
Earth Publishing Inc. (distributed by Hal Leonard,
Inc., Milwaukee, Wis.), 1986. 216pp. 0881885584.
$19.95.

Second in a series of three books defining MIDI applications. Consists of a listing of implementation charts for specific instruments as they relate to MIDI interface. Each chart provides information in thirteen categories: channel, mode, note number, velocity, touch, pitch bender, control change, program change, system exclusive, system common, system real time, aux., and notes. Instruments grouped into eight categories (digital synthesizers, hybrid synthesizers, etc.); other MIDI-related products grouped into fifteen subsequent categories which include performance controllers, sequencers, drum machines, et al. An essential book for interface information on a wide variety of existing instruments and ancillary machines.

196. De Furia, S., and J. Scacciaferro. *The MIDI System Exclusive Book*. Pompton Lakes, N.J.: Third Earth Publishing Inc., 1987. 360pp. 088188586x. $29.95.

Third in a series of three books defining MIDI applications. Technical data for customized commands used by specific manufacturers in their MIDI products. Includes major manufacturers and operational procedures.

197. *Dr. T's Model T-MIDI Interface*. Chestnut Hill, Mass.: Dr. T's Music Software, n.d. (for Commodore series computers): $89.00.

A MIDI hardware interface for
Commodore series computers; requires
sequencer software.

198. Freff. "MIDI Gear Galore: An Endless Array of
Instruments and Accessories Awaits You." *A+*, 4,2
(Feb. 1986): 35-41.

Survey of MIDI products as of early
1986. Includes information on networking, a list of manufacturers stressing
MIDI products, and journals covering
MIDI applications.

199. Garvin, Mark. "Designing a Music Recorder: Here
Are Ways to Get Started Writing Your Own MIDI
Software." *Dr. Dobb's Journal of Software Tools*,
12,5 (May 1987): 22-48.

An introduction to MIDI with
programming instructions for specialized purposes. Excellent coverage of
MIDI parameters including storage
formats, quantization, pilot tracks,
display methods, patch editors, and time
codes.

200. Heid, Jim. "Making Tracks." *Macworld*, 3,9 (Sept.
1986): 172-176.

Comparative evaluation of *MegaTrack XL*
(item 215) by MusicWorks and *Performer* (item 233) by Mark of the
Unicorn, two systems for inputting
music into the Macintosh computer by
keyboard/MIDI interface.

---- Heid, Jim. "Musical Wares." *Macworld*, 3,2 (Feb. 1986): 92-99.

> Evaluation of MIDI packages in conjunction with music editors; see main entry no. 60.

201. *IFM Interface.* Los Angeles, Calif.: Roland Corp., n.d. (for Apple IIe and IBM PC series computers): $425.00.

> A MIDI hardware interface which offers microphone input directly into a sequencer or other software program. Requires Roland's MPU-401 *MIDI Processor Unit* (item 227), Musicom software, and MIDI instrument.

202. *Keyboard Controlled Sequencer.* Chestnut Hill, Mass.: Dr. T's Music Software. 1984, 1987. (for Commodore series, Apple series, and Atari 520/1040ST computers): $149.00 to $225.00.

> An early sequencer (1984) remarkable for its flexibility and the number of popular computers which can run it. Includes recording, editing, transposing, duplicating and other features.
>
> Review:
> *Compute!*, 8,1 (Jan. 1986): 86-87.

203. Kubicky, Jay. "A MIDI project: A MIDI Interface with Software for the IBM PC." *Byte*, 11,6 (June 1986): 199-208.

Introduction to MIDI topics along with the full schematic of a MIDI hardware interface designed for an IBM PC. Includes description of accompanying software. No code is provided in the article but is available online as MIDI111.C and RXINT11.A from BYTE-Net/BIX (see *Best of BIX,* item 249).

204. Leemon, Sheldon. "More on Amiga: Software, BASIC, and IBM Compatibility." *Creative Computing*, 11,11 (Nov. 1985): 92-95.

Pithy description of the sound capabilities of Commodore's Amiga computer, including BASIC functions and software package *MusicCraft*.

205. Lehrman, Paul D. "Multitracking MIDI Master." *MacUser*, 3,12 (Dec. 1987): 180-190.

Introduction to sequencer programs and thorough evaluation of Passport's *Master Tracks Pro* (item 212).

206. Lehrman, Paul D. "Say Hello to SID: Programs for Harnessing the Music-Making Power of SID--the Commodore 64's Sound Interface Device." *High Fidelity*, 33 (Dec. 1983): 69-73.

Not available for review.

207. Levy, Steven. "MIDI Life Crisis: Can a Columnist Turn into a Rock Superhero with a Boost from the Mac?" *Macworld*, 3,9 (Sept. 1986): 27-34.

Introduction to low cost MIDI packages for the Macintosh computer. Describes the production of a "funky rock-fusion ditty" using *Assimilation MIDI Conductor, Patch Librarian, ConcertWare+MIDI,* (item 53) and *MIDI Mac* (item 220). Concludes "I have yet to actually compose any tunes to set the whole world humming (p. 34)."

208. Mace, Scott. "Electronic Orchestras in Your Living Room: MIDI Could Make 1985 the Biggest Year Yet for Computer Musicians." *InfoWorld*, 7,12 (March 25, 1985): 29-33.

Considers the impact of MIDI technology on the musical world and commercial marketplace.

209. *MacFace MIDI Interface.* Canoga Park, Calif.: Sonus, n.d. (for Apple II series and Macintosh computers): $239.00.

A MIDI hardware interface for Apple II series and Macintosh computers; requires MIDI instrument and sequencer.

210. *Macintosh MIDI Interface.* Half Moon Bay, Calif.: Passport Designs, n.d. (for Macintosh computers): $129.00.

A MIDI hardware interface for Macintosh computers; requires MIDI instrument and sequencer.

211. Massey, Howard. *The Complete Guide to MIDI*

Software. Berkeley, Calif.: Mix Bookshelf, n.d. 228pp. $19.95.

Not available for review.

212. *Master Tracks Pro,* v1.1. Half Moon Bay, Calif.: Passport Designs, 1987. (for Macintosh, Apple II series, Commodore, and IBM PC series computers): $250.00 to $395.00.

> Well designed sequencer with impressive editing and input/output features. Contains random feature "humanize" which "unquantizes" tracks for more realistic electronic performances. Will record 64 tracks with easy-to-use controls.

> Review:
> *MacUser,* 3,12 (Dec. 1987): 180-190.

213. *Masterpiece.* Canoga Park, Calif.: Sonus, ca. 1986. (for Macintosh and Atari computers): $475.00.

> A flexible and powerful sequencer which connects to standard MIDI instruments. Includes quantization and 32 tracks per sequence features.

214. McClain, Larry. "A Crescendo of Products; Apple II and MIDI Software." *A+,* 4,2 (Feb. 1986): 45-48.

> Survey of hardware and software for Apple II and Macintosh computers as of early 1986. Products include MIDI interfaces, notation and musicianship programs, and synthesizer controllers.

Followed by a "Buyer's Guide to Apple II Music Software (pp. 50-51)."

215. *MegaTrack (XL)*, v2.1. Boston, Mass.: Musicworks, 1986. (for Macintosh computers): $150.00 (495.00).

A sequencer for the Macintosh which interfaces directly with *Deluxe Music Construction Set* (item 54) for music editing. The *XL* form costs $495.00 and includes a MIDI adapter, *DMCS*, and a *MIDIWorks* utility which allows interface with either *ConcertWare* (item 53), *MusicWorks* (item 72), or *Professional Composer* (item 76). Graphic editing procedures permit quantization and onscreen editing of sequences.

Reviews:
Macworld, 3,2 (Feb. 1986): 93-99.
Macworld, 3,9 (Sept. 1986): 172-176.

216. Messick, P., and J. Battle. "Build a MIDI Input for Your Casio SK-1." *Keyboard*, 13,8 (Aug. 1987): 34-40.

Construction directions for adding a MIDI port to the Casio *SK-1* synthesizer.

217. *MIDI Pro Tool Kit.* Half Moon Bay, Calif.: Passport Designs, n.d. (for Apple II series computers): $99.95.

Language specifications and source code locations for software developers who wish to write MIDI software, and, especially, who wish to conform to

software and hardware interface
standards established by Passport
Designs.

218. *MIDI Track III.* Los Angeles, Calif.: Hybrid Arts,
n.d. (for Atari computers): $98.00.

A 16-track sequencer with edit and
transposing features; requires MIDI
hardware interface.

219. *MIDI/4 and MIDI/8 PLUS.* Half Moon Bay, Calif.:
Passport Designs, n.d. (for Apple II series and
Commodore series computers): $99.95-149.95.

Four and eight track sequencers for
Apple and Commodore computers. *The
MIDI Plus* series interfaces with
Passport Utilities (item 235) and
Polywriter (item 75) for music notation.

220. *MIDIMac Sequencer,* v3.0. Palo Alto, Calif.: Opcode
Systems, 1987. (for Macintosh computers): $250.00.

A versatile sequencer for the
Macintosh; interfaces with *Professional
Composer* (item 76) or *Deluxe Music
Construction Set* (item 54) for notation,
and with Opcode's *MIDIMac Patch Edit-
or/Librarian* (item 307) for timbral
storage. Impressive recording capabilities with highly interactive controls.

Reviews:
Macworld, 3,2 (Feb. 1986): 93-99.
Macworld, 3,12 (Dec. 1986): 109-117.

221. *MIDIMate Interface.* Los Angeles, Calif.: Hybrid Arts, n.d. (for Atari computers): $99.00.

> A MIDI hardware interface for Atari computers; requires MIDI instrument and sequencer.

222. *MIDIMerge.* Plano, Tex.: Systems Design Associates, Inc., n.d. (for IBM PC series computers): $599.00.

> Software package which allows eight MIDI instruments to simultaneously record into a sequencer. Designed to interface with *The ProMIDI Studio System* (item 246), the program will operate with selected other sequencers.

223. *MIF MIDI Interface.* Los Angeles, Calif.: Roland Corp., n.d. (for Amiga, Apple, Commodore and IBM PC series computers): $130.00.-164.00.

> A MIDI hardware interface for popular computers. Requires Roland's MPU-401 *MIDI Processing Unit* (item 227) and sequencer software.

224. Minor, David. "Music: A Buyer's Guide to Software." *Popular Computing,* 4,2 (Dec. 1984): 244.

> Description of music software (*Synthby 64, Music Construction Set*--item 54--*Musicalc 1,2, and 3, Advanced Music-system, Songwriter*--item 84--and *Orchestra 90*) and add-on cards (Mockingboard, ALF *MC1* and *MC16*, Mountain Computer, and Decillionix *DX-1*).

---- Moog, Powell, and Anderton, eds. *Sythesizers and Computers* (Keyboard Synthesizer Library). Milwaukee, Wis.: Hal Leonard Publishing Corp., 1985. iv, 129pp. 0881882917. $9.95.

> Articles on MIDI applications; see main entry no. 309.

225. Moog, Robert A. "The Soundchaser Computer Music Systems." *Byte*, 7,12 (Dec. 1982): 260-277.

> Evaluation and technical description of the Soundchaser *Computer Music Systems*.

226. Morabito, Margaret. "A MIDI Musical Package: MIDI Users Sequencer/Editor." *inCider*, 4,11 (Nov. 1986): 42ff.

> Review of MIDI products by Roland Corporation.

227. *MPU-401 MIDI Processing Unit*. Los Angeles, Calif.: Roland Corp., ca. 1985. (Computers: all popular brands with appropriate interface purchased separately): $275.00.

> A processing unit necessary for the connection of MIDI instruments to Roland interfaces and software.

228. *Music Processing System*. Los Angeles, Calif.: Roland Corporation, n.d. (for IBM PC series computers): $295.00.

An integrated software program for sequencing and editing music. Includes 8-track recording, editing, and printing support; requires interface card, MIDI hardware interface, and MIDI instrument.

---- *MusicWorks*. Lowell, Mass.: Hayden Software, 1984. (for Macintosh computers): $79.95.

A sequencer, editor, and synthesizer; see main entry no 72.

229. *Opcode Macintosh [Plus] Interface*. Palo Alto, Calif.: Opcode Systems, n.d. (for Macintosh computers): $150.00.

A MIDI hardware interface for Macintosh or Macintosh Plus computers; requires MIDI instrument and sequencer.

230. *Opcode Studio Plus II Interface*. Palo Alto, Calif.: Opcode Systems, n.d. (for Macintosh computers): $275.00.

A MIDI hardware interface for Macintosh computers which allows input of two MIDI instruments simultaneously.

231. *PC-MIDI Card*. Noteworthy (Berkeley, Calif.: Mix Bookshelf), n.d. (for IBM PC series computers): $295.00.

A MIDI hardware interface/sequencer for IBM PC series computers; requires MIDI instrument.

232. Pennycook, Bruce W. "Computer-Music Interfaces: A Survey." *ACM Computing Surveys*, 17,2 (June 1985): 267-289.

A conceptual discussion of music interface types, designs, and related problems and/or goals. Centers on three musical tasks: notation, compositional languages, and real-time performance systems. Notes that "the design requirements of musical information and performance . . . have required unique solutions," and "efforts to solve all aspects of music interface specification have exposed some general interface problems, and pointed the way toward some substantive solutions for all user interface designers (p. 286)." Bibliography.

233. *Performer*, v2.2. Cambridge, Mass.: Mark of the Unicorn, Inc., 1985, 1987 (for Macintosh computers): $295.00.

A sequencer which records and edits data streams from a MIDI instrument. Interfaces with *Professional Composer* (item 76) to produce an entire chain of play-record-notate(print)-play. Records individual or multiple tracks and supplies key signature, single or multiple meters, editing control, and quantization (with quantization level adjustable by the user). Requires MIDI hardware interface and instrument for input. Excellent manual.

Reviews:
Macworld, 3,12 (Dec. 1986): 109-117.
Macworld, 3,9 (Sept. 1986): 172-176.

---- *Personal Composer,* v2.0 (developed by Jim Miller). Honaunau, Hawaii: Jim Miller, ca.1983, 1987 (for IBM PC series computers): $495.00.

An integrated sequencer/editor software program with 32-track recording capability; see main entry no. 74.

234. *Personal Musician.* Canoga Park, Calif.: Sonus, n.d. (for Apple II series, Commodore Series, Atari 520/1040ST, IBM PC series computers): $129.00.

A medium cost sequencing program available for most popular computers. Four track record capability and MIDI hardware interface included (requires only a MIDI compatible instrument and computer).

235. *Polywriter Utilities.* Half Moon Bay, Calif.: Passport Designs, n.d. (for Apple II series, Commodore 64 computers): $149.95-169.95.

A utility software program which converts sequencer data into editor data and vice versa. Connects music editors *Polywriter* (item 75) and *Leadsheeter* (item 63) to sequencers *MIDI/4 PLUS, MIDI/8PLUS* (item 219), others.

236. Powell, R., and R. Grehan. "Four MIDI interfaces: MIDI Interfaces for the Commodore 64, IBM PC, Macintosh, and Apple II Family." *Byte*, 11,6 (June 1986): 265-272.

> Evaluation and comparison of MIDI interfaces: Syntech's *TDS-AP*, Roland's *MPU-401* (item 227), and Opcode's *MIDIMac* (item 221).

---- Powell, Roger. "The Challenge of Music Software: An Overview of the Current State of Computers in Music." *Byte*, 11,6 (June 1986): 145-150.

> Historical context of MIDI applications; see main entry no. 33.

237. *PRO-16 and PRO-24*. Northridge, Calif.: Steinberg Research, n.d. (for Commodore 64 (16 track) and Atari ST (24 track) computers): $195.00 and $295.00.

> A 16 or 24 track sequencer with editing and quantization capabilities.

238. Ruth, Clay. "Mockingboard Speech Update." *Call A.P.P.L.E.*, 8,6 (June 1985): 41-42.

> Information on updates of the *Mockingboard*, including *Mockingboard C* and *D*, with program to improve the performance of the add-on board.

239. *Sequencer Plus*, v2.0. Mamaroneck, N.Y.: Voyetra Technologies, n.d. (for IBM PC series computers): $495.00.

A large, 64-track sequencer with menu driven controls and full editing capabilities. Requires interface card, MIDI hardware interface, and MIDI instrument.

240. Sirota, Warren. "Music Programs for Computers, 1." *Guitar Player*, 21,6 (June 1987): 126-129.

General information on sequencer use by guitarists.

241. *Soundscape ProMIDI Studio*. Palo Alto, Calif.: Mimetics Corp., n.d. (for Amiga computers): $149.00.

A 16-track sequencer with input from QWERTY keyboard or MIDI instrument. Includes synthesizer and editing features; requires MIDI hardware interface.

242. Swearingen, Donald. "A MIDI Recorder: Store and Play Back Keyboard Music with Your IBM PC." *Byte*, 10,11 (Fall 1985): 127-138.

Development of a MIDI software program in FORTH, written for the IBM PC and Roland's MPU-401 *M I D I Processing Unit* (item 227). Provides background on MIDI, the MPU-401 processor, and code.

243. Swearingen, Donald. "MIDI programming: Processing the MPU-401 track data stream." *Byte*, 11,6 (June 1986): 211-224.

Turbo Pascal programs designed to process data streams from MIDI interfaces. Excellent coverage of the major MIDI utilities with clear directions for programmers. Programs described in article are available online from BYTEnet Listings (617-861-9764) or BIX (Byte Information eXchange).

244. *Texture*, v2.0. Beekman, N.Y.: Musicsoft, n.d. (for IBM PC series and Amiga computers): $299.00.

A sequencer for IBM and Amiga computers notable for its storage capabilities (72,000 notes). Includes tape sync, overdub, and note-by-note editing.

245. *The Music Shop-MIDI.* Half Moon Bay, Calif.: Passport Designs, n.d. (for Commodore series computers): $149.95.

An integrated editor/sequencer package for the Commodore computer. In conjunction with a MIDI hardware interface and instrument, scores may be input directly from the instrument, edited onscreen, and printed on a dot-matrix printer. Will handle up to 20 pages of music in volatile (=RAM) memory.

246. *The ProMIDI Studio System.* Plano, Tex.: System Design Associates, Inc., n.d. (for IBM PC series computers): $599.99.

A sequencer with open-ended storage capacity based upon the hard disk memory of the IBM PC (*ProMIDI* will record real time information direct to disk). Contains sixteen-track recording capability, full editing and playback features, and a built-in file librarian. Includes MIDI hardware interface.

---- Yavelow, Christopher. "Top of the Charts: On Stage and in the Studio, the Mac is Number One with Music Professionals." *Macworld*, 4,8 (Aug. 1987): 138-145.

Examples of MIDI-based studios; see main entry no. 44.

V. Programming:
Languages, Code, Software Design, and Artificial Intelligence

247. Abbott, G., and C. Loy. "Programming Languages for Computer Music Synthesis, Performance, and Composition." *ACM Computing Surveys*, 17,2 (June 1985): 235-262.

Survey of programming languages developed for synthesis, performance, notation, and composition. Includes background coverage of problems associated with traditional music notation and language design, concluding "common practice notation presents a musical artifact in a form that mixes objective dimensions . . . with deeply embedded, and often unarticulated, knowledge of musical style and history (p. 242)." Offers succinct descriptions of low- and high-level programming languages; concludes by defining the need for a combination of both in a single, intelligent language such as PROLOG. Bibliography.

248. Adams, Christopher. "Sound Table: Fast Sound Effects From BASIC." *Creative Computing*, 9,7 (July 1983): 188-192.

A shape table created by machine language (*Soundtable*) with accompanying and controlling BASIC program (*Soundmaker*). Produces 256 waveforms with Apple computers.

---- Barger, Victor. "Sketch the Wave." *Nibble Mac*, 2,8 (Dec. 1987): 40-42ff.

BASIC code for waveform construction; see main entry no. 278.

---- Bartle, Barton K. *Computer Software in Music and Music Education: A Guide*. Metuchen, N.J.: Scarecrow Press, 1987. xiv, 252pp. 0810820560.

Bibliography of software items to be published in early 1988.

---- Bateman, Wayne. *Introduction to Computer Music* (A Wiley-Science Publication). New York: John Wiley and Sons, 1980. vii, 314pp. 0471052663. $20.00.

Manual on composition with valuable appendices on programming in BASIC and FORTRAN; see main entry no. 47.

249. *Best of BIX* (bulletin board for Amiga, Apple, Macintosh, IBM, other popular computers). *Byte*. regular feature, 1985 to date.

Listings of programs available through Byte's Information Exchange, an online, public domain software service (membership required: BIX, One Phoenix Mill Lane, Peterborough, N.H. 03458, 603/924-9281; one time fee of $25.00). Includes music programs, often ones discussed in current articles.

---- Bonaventura, Antony P. *Making Music with Microprocessors* (Radio Shack Publications). Blue Ridge Summit, Pa.: Tab Books Inc., 1984. viii, 286pp. 0830607293. $16.95.

Assembly language programs for computer synthesis; see main entry no. 279.

250. Boudreaux, Paul J. "Getting into Integer BASIC." *Microcomputing*, 8,7 (July 1984): 102-105.

Description of the *Music* machine language program located within Integer BASIC on the Apple II Plus.

---- "Buyer's Guide to Music Hardware and Software (1986); Regardless of Musical Talent, Your Family Can Make Beautiful Music." *Family Computing*, 4,8 (Aug. 1986): 36-40.

Survey of popular music software ca. 1986; see main entry no. 184.

---- Chamberlin, Hal. "Advanced Real-Time Music Synthesis Techniques." *Byte*, 5,4 (April 1980): 70-94ff.

BASIC and assembly language programs for D/A conversion; see main entry no. 282.

251. Clough, John. "TEMPO: a Composer's Programming Language." *Perspectives of New Music*, 9,1 (1970): 113-125.

Explanation of TEMPO (=Transformational Electronic Music Process Organizer), a composition and performance language developed at Oberlin (1969 on). Program based on a three stage process of compilation, sorting, and performance.

252. Clynes, Manfred, ed. *Music, Mind, and Brain: The Neuropsychology of Music*. New York: Plenum Press, 1982. xii, 430pp. 0306409089.

Selected papers (21) from the third Workshop on the Physical and Neuropsychological Foundations of Music held in Ossiach, Austria, 1980. Articles by leading figures such as Minsky, Roederer, Deutsch, Balzano, and others exhibit exceptionally high degrees of intuition and creativity. Organized into three parts: I, Concerning the Language of Music, II, Music and Neurobiological Function, and III, Concerning Music and Computers. Terhardt's article "Impact of Computers on Music" provides a superb organization of the field, a useful introductory reading. Recorded sound sheet included; concludes with author and subject indexes.

253. Coker, Frank. "Random Music: Generate Music
With a Special Twist--Just Type in these Four Little
Listings." *inCider*, 2,12 (Dec. 1984): 93-96.

> BASIC programs which create random
> pitches within a three octave chromatic
> scale; code also produces accompanying
> graphic displays.

---- Dodge, C., and C. Bahn. "Musical Fractals:
Mathematical Formulas Can Produce Musical as
well as Graphic Fractals." *Byte*, 11,6 (June 1986):
185-196.

> Programs for fractal composition; see
> main entry no. 55.

---- Dolen, William K. "Your Well Tempered Music
Synthesizer." *Call A.P.P.L.E.*, 9,2 (Feb. 1986): 14-16.

> BASIC program for producing historical
> temperaments on the Apple computer;
> see main entry no. 288.

---- Dolen, William K. "Making (Sound) Waves with the
Macintosh." *Call A.P.P.L.E.*, 8,11 (Dec. 1985): 40-44.

> Software code for producing complex
> waveforms on the Macintosh; see main
> entry no. 289.

254. Fink, Michael. "The Well-Tempered Apple."
Creative Computing, 9,7 (July 1983): 196-198.

> Programming method for extending the
> frequency range of the Apple computer

using delay techniques in machine
language. Provides a simple BASIC
program for accessing the delay sub-
routine.

255. Foerster, H., and J. Beauchamp, eds. *Music by
Computers.* New York: John Wiley and Sons, Inc.,
1969. xv, 139pp. 69-19244.

Papers read at the 1966 Computer
Conference Session, "Computers in
Music." Divided into three parts as I,
Programs and Systems, II, Algorithms in
Composition, and III, Aesthetics. Seminal but useful articles by Beauchamp on
time-variant harmonic analysis, Hiller
on compositional techniques, Mathews
and Rosler on graphics, and Strang on
imperfection in computer music.
References at the end of each of the 9
articles.

256. Fudge, Don. "Fudge It!: Tuning Up Your Apple: Add
Melody and a Little Charm to Your Programs with
Apple Music." *inCider*, 3,6 (June 1985): 53-60.

BASIC programs which turn the Apple
II keyboard into a piano-like instrument.

---- Garvin, Mark. "Designing a Music Recorder: Here
Are Ways to Get Started Writing Your Own MIDI
Software." *Dr. Dobb's Journal of Software Tools*,
12,5 (May 1987): 22-48.

Programming instructions for MIDI
applications; see main entry no. 199.

257. Gibson, Don Phillip. "Tandy Tunes: Make Beautiful Music Together with Your Tandy 1000." *80 Micro*, 83 (Dec. 1986): 89-93.

> Introduction to music programming for the Tandy 1000 computer. Employs "Play" statement from BASIC in a sample program which sounds an excerpt from Bach's *E-flat-major Trio Sonata* (B W V 525) for organ.

258. Gourlay, John S. "A Language for Music Printing." *Communications of the ACM*, 29,5 (May 1986): 388-401.

> Theoretical development of a high-level language to produce publication quality scores. System allows for expression of concurrency and two-dimensionality. Bibliography.

---- Gross, Dorothy S. "A Set of Computer Programs to Aid in Music Analysis." Ph.D. dissertation, Indiana University. Ann Arbor: UMI Press, 1975. vi, 358pp.

> Development and code for six analytical programs; see main entry no. 59.

259. Gustafsson, Roland. "Ensoniq Sounds." *A+*, 5,1 (Jan. 1987): 52.

> BASIC program demonstrating sound capabilities of the Apple IIGS synthesizer/computer.

---- Heid, Jim. "Musical Wares." *Macworld*, 3,2 (Feb. 1986): 93-99.

> Analysis and design of eleven software packages for sequencing and editing music; see main entry no. 60.

260. Jainschigg, John. "Apple Harmony." *Family Computing*, 4,8 (Aug. 1986): 62-64.

> Machine language subroutine which allows an Apple II computer to play three-part harmony. Includes a simple conversion table for relating notes to language numbers.

261. Jefferys, Douglas W. "Nibble Duet: Tired of Your Apple's Sound?" *Nibble*, 6,12 (Dec. 1985): 137-141.

> BASIC and assembly language programs for creating two-voice polyphony on the Apple II computer.

262. Katz, Robert. "Converting Pitch to Frequency." *Byte*, 6,2 (Feb. 1981): 92-94.

> Frequency conversion program for the Hewlett-Packard calculator written in Reverse Polish Notation.

---- Kubicky, Jay. "A MIDI project: A MIDI Interface with Software for the IBM PC." *Byte*, 11,6 (June 1986): 199-208.

Description and online information about MIDI software and design; see main entry no. 203.

263. Latimer, Joey. "Microtones." *Family Computing*, (intermittent monthly series): Sept. 1983 to date.

Monthly series of BASIC programs which play a wide variety of popular songs. Latimer's programs are notable for the breadth of code offered (a single program is supplied in multiple listings, each for a specific microcomputer) and for the variety of musical approaches (canons, sing-alongs, etc.).

---- Mathews, M., and F. Moore. "Computers and Future Music." *Science*, 183,4122 (Jan. 25, 1974): 263-268.

Discussion of composition languages Music V and Groove; see main entry no. 24.

264. Mathews, Miller, Moore, et al. *The Technology of Computer Music*. Cambridge, Mass.: MIT Press, 1969/1974. 188pp. 0262130505.

One of the foundations of the field, an early study defining the mathematical and engineering basis of computer music. Emphasis on the technical construction of algorithms employing FORTRAN language. Constructed in textbook format with reinforcing problems for the student at the end of each chapter. Essential text for the serious musician interested in design-

ing his or her own hardware and software. Includes notes at ends of
chapters, appendices on acoustic and
mathematical topics, and indexes of
terms and names.

265. Mefford, Michael J. "A DOS Music Generator." *PC
Magazine*, 6,8 (April 28, 1987): 297ff.

Programming instructions for creating
sound parameters on the PC directly out
of DOS. Includes terms and commands.

---- *MIDI Pro Tool Kit*. Half Moon Bay, Calif.: Passport
Designs. (for Apple II series computers), n.d.
$99.95.

Language specifications and source code
locations for software developers who
wish to write MIDI software, and,
especially, who wish to conform to
software and hardware interfaces
established by Passport Designs; see
main entry no. 217.

---- Morse, Raymond W. "Use of Microcomputer
Graphics to Aid in the Analysis of Music." DMA
Thesis, University of Oregon. Ann Arbor: UMI
Press, 1985. x, 180pp.

Development of programs to analyze
music; see main entry no. 68.

266. Murken, Hinrich. "Translingo." *Creative
Computing*, 9,7 (July 1983): 117-121.

A system for assigning letters to musical symbols (Translingo="word forming principle of the English language"). Useful for inputting music in alphanumeric code.

267. Nelson, Randolph. "A Graphics Text Editor for Music, Part 1: Structure of the Editor." *Byte*, 5,4 (April 1980): 124-138.

Overview of design characteristics of a music editor with explanations of musical symbols, input and data structure areas, and onscreen design.

---- Orlofsky, Thomas P. "Computer Music: A Design Tutorial." *Byte*, 6,3 (March 1981): 317-332.

Assembly language programs for digital generation; see main entry no. 316.

---- Pennycook, Bruce W. "Computer-Music Interfaces: A Survey." *ACM Computing Surveys*, 17,2 (June 1985): 267-289.

Language design and requirements for computer interface; see main entry no. 232.

268. Perkins, Bob. "Modification of Celestial Music." *Creative Computing*, 9,7 (July 1983): 202-204.

Revision of earlier program by Leo Christopherson allowing music input into an Apple computer by means of machine language.

269. Ramella, Richard. "Sound Advice for the 4/4P." *80 Micro*, 4,23 (Nov. 1985): 341-343.

> Primitive programs possible on the Radio Shack 4/4P computers.

---- Roads, C., and J. Strawn, eds. *Foundations of Computer Music*. Cambridge, Mass.: MIT Press, 1985 (hardback), 1987 (paperback). xiii, 712pp. 0262181142h, 0262680513p.

> Articles on software design and languages; see main entry no. 324.

270. Roads, Curtis. "Research in Music and Artificial Intelligence." *ACM Computing Surveys*, 17,2 (June 1985): 163-190.

> Well designed introduction into artificial intelligence, computers, and music. Begins with a two-fold definition of AI (cognitive science and/or applied AI), proceeds to a brief historical summary of "intelligent machines." Divides central AI problems into four musical areas: composition, performance, music theory, and sound processing. Considers the current state of research and development for each area. Concludes with speculations about future trends and the processes of learning in music systems. Excellent first reading for the serious musician interested in AI. Useful bibliography.

---- Russell, Roberta C. "A Set of Microcomputer Programs to Aid in the Analysis of Atonal Music."

DMA Thesis, University of Oregon. Ann Arbor: UMI Press, 1983. ix, 157pp.

> Software design and code for two analytical programs; see main entry no. 81.

271. Smith, David L. "Nibble Maestro." *Nibble*, 6,7 (July 1985): 52-61.

> BASIC programs for music notation and graphic display; written for the Apple II computer. Good introduction into musical programming in Applesoft BASIC.

272. Stradler, Neal. "Exploring Music with Logo." *Computing Teacher*, 12,6 (March 1985): 16-18.

> Instruction to LOGO programming with sample code which produces monophonic songs.

---- Swearingen, Donald. "A MIDI Recorder: Store and Play Back Keyboard Music with Your IBM PC." *Byte*, 10,11 (Fall 1985): 127-138.

> MIDI programming in FORTH; see main entry no. 242.

---- Swearingen, Donald. "MIDI Programming: Processing the MPU-401 Track Data Stream." *Byte*, 11,6 (June 1986): 211-224.

> TurboPascal MIDI programming; see main entry no. 243.

273. Tubb, Phil. "Musical Subroutines" *Creative Computing*, 8,3 (March 1982): 124-132.

> Theoretical development of a musical language using subroutines with traditional titles (=CALL Verse, CALL Chorus, etc.).

---- Wallace, Robert L. "Your Sort of Computer Program!" *Music Educators Journal*, 71,5 (Jan. 1985): 33-36.

> BASIC program for education use; see main entry no. 175.

---- Whitney, John. *Digital Harmony: On the Complementarity of Music and Visual Art.* Peterborough, N.H.: Byte Books by McGraw-Hill, 1980. 235pp. 007070015X. $21.95.

> Description of Pascal programs employed for compositional uses; see main entry no. 87.

274. Williams, D., and D. Bowers. *Designing Computer-Based Instruction for Music and the Arts.* Bellevue, Wash.: Temporal Acuity Products, Inc., n.d. 240pp. $55.00.

> A programming method constructed for the Apple II series computers. Employs top-down code structure and includes sample program shells. Text provides specific discussion of CBI software design.

275. Wittlich, Schaffer, and Babb. *Microcomputers and Music*. Englewood Cliffs, N.J.: Prentice-Hall, 1986. xiii, 321pp. 0135805155.

The first major study designed to teach music programming. Employs a "top-down" approach toward structured code which complements the design of BASIC well. Requires some prior background in BASIC but provides a tutorial "Guide to BASIC" as Appendix A. Prepares the reader for major tasks including data structures, CAI drills, graphics design and manipulation, and sound generation. Programs will run on Apple, IBM, and Commodore computers using standard BASIC languages; however there are numerous errors in the code supplied (see the review listed below for a partial list). Exercises at ends of chapters reinforce concepts; solutions are offered in the final Appendix. An essential text for the music/computer programmer, in great need of a revised and corrected version. Index of names and terms.

Review:
Journal of Music Theory, 31,1 (Spring 1987): 157-163.

---- Zimmermann, Mark. "A Beginner's Guide to Spectral Analysis, Part 1: Tiny Timesharing Music." *Byte,* 6,2 (Feb. 1981): 68-90.

BASIC programs for Fourier analysis; see main entry no. 335.

---- Zimmermann, Mark. "A Beginner's Guide to Spectral Analysis, Part 2." *Byte*, 6,3 (March 1981): 166-198.

Assembly language programs for spectral analysis; see main entry no. 336.

276. Zimmerman, S. Scott. "Counting on Sixteen Fingers." *Nibble*, 6,7 (July 1985): 75-84.

An introduction to assembly language programming with construction of a sample program, "Apple Organ."

VI. Synthesis:
Acoustics, Voice Libraries, and Sampling

---- Abbott, G., and C. Loy. "Programming Languages for Computer Music Synthesis, Performance, and Composition." *ACM Computing Surveys*, 17,2 (June 1985): 235-262.

Languages for synthesis purposes; see main entry no. 247.

277. Banes, Vince. "Audio-Frequency Analyzer: Build IBM PC Accessories to Analyze Your Stereo." *Byte*, 10,1 (Jan. 1985): 223-250.

Construction of a DAC, ADC, and VCO designed to chart the frequency response of a stereo system with aid of an IBM PC. Finished product employs BASIC programs to run tests. Full schematics, programs, diagrams, and information on calibration.

278. Barger, Victor. "Sketch the Wave." *Nibble Mac*, 2,8 (Dec. 1987): 40-42ff.

> A simple but flexible BASIC program for waveform construction and editing. Makes excellent use of windowing capabilities and offers the home programmer useful experience in programming code into a Macintosh computer.

---- Bateman, Wayne. *Introduction to Computer Music* (A Wiley-Interscience Publication). New York: John Wiley and Sons, 1980. vii, 314pp. 0471052663. $20.00.

> Technical explanation of synthesis techniques; see main entry no. 47.

279. Bonaventura, Antony P. *Making Music with Microprocessors* (Radio Shack Publications). Blue Ridge Summit, Pa.: Tab Books Inc., 1984. viii, 286pp. 0830607293. $16.95.

> A practical "how-to" book dealing with fundamental principles of computer sound generation and elementary digital synthesis. Background chapters on music theory, acoustics, and circuit design; major topics consist of writing assembly language programs which perform music on the computer and the creation of a computer-assisted synthe-sizer. "Recommended readings" at the end of each chapter offer additional information. Index of terms.

Review:
Computer Music Journal, 9,4 (Winter
1985): 66-67.

280. *Caged Artist Editor/Librarian Programs.* Chestnut
Hill, Mass.: Dr. T's Music Software, n.d. (for Apple
and Commodore series computers): $99.00.

Software programs for storing, organizing and editing waveforms. Available
for Yamaha *DX21, 27,* and *100,* Oberheim
Matrix-6, and Roland *JX-8P* synthesizers;
require MIDI hardware interfaces.

281. *Casio Programmer Librarian.* Canoga Park, Calif.:
Sonus, n.d. (for Commodore series computers):
$129.95.

Software program for the storage,
editing, and organizing of waveforms.
Compatible with Casio series synthesizers; requires MIDI hardware interface.

282. Chamberlin, Hal. "Advanced Real-Time Music
Synthesis Techniques." *Byte,* 5,4 (April 1980): 70-
94ff.

Theory and practice of microcomputer
synthesis using D/A conversion.
Excellent discussion of waveform
computation, scanning and filling
waveform tables, and amplitude. BASIC
and assembly language programs
provided which illustrate concepts.
Bibliography.

283. Ciarcia, Steve. "Sound Off." *Byte*, 4,7 (July 1979): 34-51.

> Technical discussion of sound chips by Texas Instruments (SN76477) and General Instrument (AY-3-8910) along with schematics and assembly language programs necessary for connecting them to microcomputers.

---- *ConcertWare+*. Stanford, Calif.: Great Wave Software, 1985. (for Macintosh computers): $69.95.

> Integrated sequencer, editor, and synthesizer; see main entry no. 53.

284. Crombie, David. *The New Complete Synthesizer: A Comprehensive Guide to the World of Electronic Music*. New York: Omnibus Press, 1986. 112pp. 0711907013. $12.95.

> A revision and updating of Crombie's earlier *The Complete Synthesizer* (1982). Introduces synthesizer and computer sound generation with clear, easy to understand text. Accompanied by numerous diagrams, pictures, and references to popular artists who make use of the synthesizer. Includes chapters on computers and music, interfacing, MIDI, and glossary of electronic and computer terms.

285. *CZ Patch Editor/Librarian*. Chestnut Hill, Mass.: Dr. T's Music Software, n.d. (for Commodore series and Atari ST computers): $99.00.

Software programs for storing, organizing, and editing waveforms. Designed for use with Casio series synthesizers; require MIDI hardware interfaces.

286. *CZ Rider.* Chestnut Hill, Mass.: Dr. T's Music Software, n.d. (for Apple and Commodore series computers): $99.00.

A software program which permits construction of up to 8-stage envelopes. Allows editing and playback capabilities with Casio *CZ* synthesizer and MIDI hardware interface.

287. De Furia, Steve. *The Secrets of Analog to Digital Synthesis.* Rutherford, N.J.: Third Earth Productions, 1986. 122pp. 0881885169.

Not available for review.

---- Dodge, C., and T. Jerse. *Computer Music: Synthesis, Composition, and Performance.* New York: Schirmer Books, 1985. xi, 383pp. 002873100X.

Detailed consideration of synthesis techniques; see main entry no. 56.

288. Dolen, William K. "Your Well Tempered Music Synthesizer." *Call A.P.P.L.E.*, 9,2 (Feb. 1986): 14-16.

Explanation of five tuning systems (equal temperament, just intonation, Pythagorean tuning, meantone temperament, and Silbermann temperament) with a BASIC program capable of reproducing same.

289. Dolen, William K. "Making (Sound) Waves with the Macintosh." *Call A.P.P.L.E.*, 8,11 (Dec. 1985): 40-44.

Brief discussion of Fourier analysis, the harmonic series, and a model program constructed to produce a complex waveform and accompanying graph.

290. *DX Android.* Los Angeles, Calif.: Hybrid Arts, n.d. (for Atari computers): $199.95.

A software program for storing, editing, and organizing waveforms. Employs a simple form of artificial intelligence in order to create waveforms randomly. Compatible with Yamaha DX and TX series, requires a MIDI hardware interface.

291. *DX Connect.* Palo Alto, Calif.: Mimetics, n.d. (for IBM PC series computers): $149.95.

A software program for storing, editing, and organizing waveforms. Compatible with Yamaha DX and TX synthesizers, requires MIDI hardware interface.

292. *DX Patch Editor/Librarian.* Chestnut Hill, Mass.: Dr. T's Music Software, n.d. (for Apple and Commodore series computers): $99.00.

A software program for the storage, organization, and editing of waveforms.

Interfaces with Yamaha DX series synthesizers, requires MIDI hardware interface.

293. *DX-1 Sound Sampling System.* Sunnyvale, Calif.: Decillionix, n.d. (for Apple II series computers): $249.00.

A digital sound sampler in software form for the Apple computer. Allows the recording, editing, and playing of waveforms in a variety of formats.

294. *DX-TX Support Programs.* Canoga Park, Calif.: Sonus, n.d. (for Commodore series computers): $139.95-149.95.

Software programs which allow visual display of waveforms created on Yamaha synthesizers *DX7, TX7, DX21, 27,* and *100.*

295. *DX-TX-LP.* Canoga Park, Calif.: Sonus, n.d. (for Commodore series computers): $159.00.

Software programs for storing, organizing, and editing waveforms. Compatible with Yamaha DX and TX series; require MIDI hardware interfaces.

296. *DXLIB.* Noteworthy Systems (Berkeley, Calif.: Mix Bookshelf), n.d. (for IBM PC series computers): $79.00

A software program for storing, editing,
and organizing waveforms. Compatible
with Yamaha *DX7* synthesizer; requires
MIDI hardware interface.

297. *Envelope Construction* (developed by D. Williams,
D. Braught, and J. Schulze). Bellevue, Wash.:
Temporal Acuity Products, Inc., ca. 1980. (for
Apple II series computers): $125.00.

An experimenter program for the Apple
II series computers. Allows for control
of time, amplitude, and harmonic
contents of a waveform and accompanying three-dimensional imagery.
DAC board required.

298. *Envelope Shaper* (developed by D. Williams, D.
Braught, and J. Schulze). Bellevue, Wash.:
Temporal Acuity Products, Inc., ca. 1980. (for
Apple II series computers): $75.00.

An accompanying program to *Music
Composer* (item 69), *Envelope Shaper*
provides basic synthesis for *Music
Composer* files. Permits control over
timbre, tempo, transposition, and
repetition in an interactive, real-time
setting. DAC board required.

299. *Explore Temperament: The MIRAGE Multi-
Temperament Disk* (developed by D. Lord).
Durham, N.H.: Upward Concepts, 1987. (for the
Ensoniq Mirage Sound Sampler): price
unavailable.

A software "monochord" for the Ensoniq sound sampler. Allows the *Ensoniq Mirage* to play in ten historical tunings including Pythagorean, meantone, Silbermann, Werckmeister, Kirnberger, and varieties of equal temperament. Permits the setting of the tonic to any chromatic pitch, a useful feature for just intonations.

300. Gordon, John W. "System Architectures for Computer Music." *ACM Computing Surveys*, 17,2 (June 1985): 191-233.

Overview of hardware design for computer and synthesis systems. Written for the engineer or computer scientist, the article remains sufficiently clear to the technically oriented musician to serve as a tutor in basic synthesizer design and computerized methods of control. Specific discussion of algorithms, DAC and ADC converters, and existing synthesizer systems. Concludes with speculation on the impact of VLSI (=Very Large Scale Integration) on synthesized sound. Bibliography.

301. Grey, John M. *An Exploration of Musical Timbre* (Center for Computer Research in Music and Acoustics, STAN-M-2). Palo Alto, Calif.: Department of Music: Stanford University, 1975. 133pp. 76-377790.

A computerized study of timbre emphasizing analysis-based additive synthesis. Includes excellent historical

review of timbre research, discussion of
the present state of research (as of 1975)
and a series of four behavioral
experiments illuminating the nature of
timbre as well as distinctions between
acoustical and synthesized tones. The
author suggests that "naturalistic tones
can be synthesized from a vastly
simplified set of physical properties"
and produces such a model. Three
appendices include detailed descriptions of analysis-based additive
synthesis, graphical techniques, and
multidimensional scaling techniques.
An important introduction to the topic
for computer and synthesizer purposes.
Excellent bibliography.

302. *Hippo 8-Bit Audio Sampler.* Hippopotamus
Software Inc., (Berkeley, Calif.: Mix Bookshelf),
n.d. (for Atari ST computers): $139.95.

An 8-bit digital sampler in software
form for Atari computers. Records,
edits, and synthesizes up to four channels of sound; all hardware included.

303. *Hybrid Arts DX Editor/Librarian.* Los Angeles,
Calif.: Hybrid Arts, n.d. (for Atari computers):
$59.50.

A software program which edits, stores,
and organizes waveforms. Compatible
with Yamaha DX series; requires Hybrid
Arts MIDI interface.

---- *IFM-APL Interface for the Apple IIe, IBM PC.* Los

Angeles, Calif.: Roland Corp., n.d. (for Apple IIe computers): $425.00.

An interface which offers microphone input into either the Apple IIe or IBM PC; see main entry no. 201.

304. Kendall, Gary Stephen. "Theory and Application of Digital Filtering in Computer-Generated Music." Ph.D. dissertation, University of Texas, Austin. Ann Arbor: UMI Press, 1982.

Not available for review.

305. Levitt, David. "Pushing the Sound Envelope: These Programs Make It Easier for Musical Novices to Make Music." *Dr. Dobb's Journal of Software Tools*, 12,5 (May 1987): 16-19.

General discussion of the effects of performing gestures on musical timbre and a brief consideration of MIDI and algorithmic principles of composition.

306. *Macnifty Audio Digitizer*. Macnifty (Berkeley, Calif.: Mix Bookshelf), ca. 1986. (for Macintosh computers): $199.95.

A digital sound sampler in software form for Macintosh computers. Offers recording, editing, and playback capabilities and includes a spectral analyzer.

---- Manning, Peter. *Electronic and Computer Music*. Oxford: Clarendon Press, 1985. 291pp. 0193119188. $29.95.

Historical and descriptive account of the synthesizer; see main entry no. 23.

---- Mathews, Miller, Moore, et al. *The Technology of Computer Music.* Cambridge, Mass.: MIT Press, 1969/1974. 188pp. 0262130505.

Mathematical and theoretical basis of synthesizer design; see main entry no. 264.

307. *MIDIMac Patch Librarians.* Palo Alto, Calif.: Opcode Systems, n.d. (for Macintosh computers): $100.00-250.00.

A series of software programs for storing, editing, and organizing waveforms. Individual programs compatible with Yamaha, Casio, Oberheim, Roland, and Korg synthesizers; require MIDI hardware interfaces.

308. *Mirage and Prophet Sonic Editors.* Sonic Access (Berkeley, Calif.: Mix Bookshelf), n.d. (for Commodore series computers): $149.00-225.00.

Software programs which store, organize, and edit waveforms. Designed for the *Ensoniq Mirage* and *Sequential Prophet* samplers in conjunction with Commodore computers and MIDI hardware interfaces.

309. Moog, Powell, and Anderton, eds. *Synthesizers and*

Computers (Keyboard Synthesizer Library).
Milwaukee, Wis.: Hal Leonard Publishing Corp.,
1985. iv, 129pp. 0881882917. $9.95.

A collection of 22 articles which first
appeared in *Keyboard Magazine* from
1978 to 1984. Practical and lucid
explanations of modern digital techniques by major figures such as
Chowning, Mathews, Moog, and others.
Three sections cover digital synthesis,
home computer applications, and MIDI
interfaces. Craig Anderton's article
"Computer Literacy for Musicians"
serves as a practical first reading for
the prospective computer music
afficionado. An appendix provides the
specifications for MIDI 1.0 as of 1983;
index of names and terms.

310. Moog, Powell, Rhea, Porcaro, et al. *Synthesizer
Basics* (Keyboard Synthesizer Library).
Milwaukee, Wis.: Hal Leonard Publishing Corp.,
1984. vii, 111pp. 0881882895. $9.95.

A collection of articles appearing in
Keyboard Magazine from 1975 to 1980.
Considers analog and voltage control
techniques in practical contexts for
composers and performers. Includes
four sections on perspectives
(=introduction), basic concepts and
components, sound systems and
accessories, and recording and
"specmanship." Contains an early
article on MIDI interfacing, a brief
bibliography, glossary, index, and
"frequently asked questions and
answers about synthesizers."

311. Moog, Robert A. "Digital Music Synthesis: The
     Many Different Shapes of the Waveform of the
     Present." *Byte*, 11,6 (June 1986): 155-168.

     Summary of commercially available
     synthesizers, placed in historical pers-
     pective. Includes descriptions of Casio,
     Yamaha, Synergy, Kurzweil, and soft-
     ware generated synthesis systems.
     Concludes with trends for the future.

312. Moorer, James A. *On the Loudness of Complex,
     Time-Variant Tones* (Center for Computer
     Research in Music and Acoustics STAN-M-4). Palo
     Alto, Calif.: Department of Music, Stanford
     University, 1975. 18pp.

     Not available for review.

313. Moorer, James A. *On the Segmentation and
     Analysis of Continuous Musical Sound by Digital
     Computer* (Center for Computer Research in Music
     and Acoustics, STAN-M-3). Palo Alto, Calif.:
     Department of Music, Stanford University, 1975.
     165pp. 76-377789.

     A seminal study considering the
     transcription of sound by digital
     computer. Employs filtering, predic-
     tion, and intermediate level processing
     algorithms to transfer acoustic and
     synthesized sound into conventional
     notation. Severe restrictions are placed
     upon input sounds because of the
     filtering and analytical systems
     employed. Appendices such as the
     heterodyne filter, digital filters, and
     bibliography.

314. *MusicSoft Drum Machine Data Managers.*
Beekman, N.Y.: MusicSoft, n.d. (for Apple and IBM
serie computers): $60.00.

> Software programs for storing and
> organizing drum patterns. Designed for
> Yamaha and Roland drum machines;
> MIDI hardware interfaces required.

---- *MusicWorks.* Lowell, Mass.: Hayden Software, 1984.
(for Macintosh computers): $79.95.

> An integrated software program with
> editor, sequencer, and synthesizer; see
> main entry no. 72.

315. *Oasis.* Los Angeles, Calif.: Hybrid Arts, n.d. (for
Atari computers): $93.50.

> A software program for editing, storing,
> and organizing waveforms. Compatible
> with *Ensoniq Mirage* sampler; requires
> MIDI hardware interface.

316. Orlofsky, Thomas P. "Computer Music: A Design
Tutorial." *Byte*, 6,3 (March 1981): 317-332.

> Design of a simple program-controlled,
> digital tone generator. Includes
> schematics, flowcharts, and assembly
> language programs.

317. *Passport MIDI Voice Librarians.* Half Moon Bay,
Calif.: Passport Designs, n.d. (for Apple II series,
Commodore, and IBM series computers): $69.95-
125.00.

A series of software programs which
store and organize waveforms. Specific
packages available for Yamaha, Casio,
Korg, Oberheim, and Roland synthesizers; the Roland *JX-8P Editor/Li-
brarian* version offers editing features
as well. Require MIDI hardware
interfaces.

318. *Patch Master.* Mamaroneck, N.Y.: Voyetra
Technologies, n.d. (for IBM PC series computers):
$149.00.

A software program for editing, storing,
and organizing waveforms. Suitable for
many popular synthesizers; requires
MIDI hardware interface.

---- *Personal Composer,* v2.0 (developed by Jim Miller):
Honaunau, Hawaii: Jim Miller, n.d. (for IBM PC
series computers): $495.00.

An integrated editor, sequencer, and
synthesizer for the IBM; see main entry
no. 74.

319. Pierce, John R. *The Science of Musical Sound*
(Scientific American Library). New York:
Scientific American Books, Inc., 1983. xii, 242pp.
0716715082.

Considers major acoustical topics with
an impressive historical and interdisci-
plinary scope. Particularly useful
chapters include those on consonance
(Helmhotz's conception), harmony (as
defined by Rameau), architectural

acoustics, and an appendix "Computer generation of sound." Numerous diagrams, pictures, and graphics complement the text which offers a blend of technical information and revealing anecdotes (often concerning major 20th-century musicians). Appendices, index, and accompanying records illustrate major points. An excellent introduction into acoustics for the computer oriented musician.

320. Powell, Steven. "The ABCs of Synthesizers." *Music Educators Journal*, 73,4 (Dec. 1987): 27-31.

A well written introduction into synthesizer and computer usages as of early 1987. Includes brief and accurate descriptions of synthesis principles, digital sampling, and MIDI interfaces. A good first reading for the educator or musician just becoming interested in synthesizers or MIDI.

321. *Pro-Creator*. Northridge, Calif.: Steinberg Research, n.d. (for Atari computers): $240.00.

A software program for storing, editing, and organizing waveforms. Compatible with Yamaha DX and TX synthesizers; requires MIDI hardware interface.

322. *PROLIB*. Hollywood, Calif.: Club MIDI Software, n.d. (for IBM PC series computers): $99.95.

A software program for storing, editing, and organizing waveforms. Compatible

with many popular synthesizers; requires MIDI hardware interface.

323. Risset, C., and M. Mathews. "Analysis of Musical-
Instrument Tones; with Biographical Sketches."
Physics Today, 22,2 (Feb. 1969): 23-30.

General discussion of timbral analysis
with special attention given to trumpet
and violin tones. Considers the use of
computers in both the analysis and
synthesis of traditional instrument
timbres. Bibliography.

324. Roads, C., and J. Strawn, eds. *Foundations of
Computer Music*. Cambridge, Mass.: MIT Press, 1985
(hardback), 1987 (paperback). xiii, 712pp.
0262181142h, 0262680513p.

A collection of 36 articles first
appearing in *Computer Music Journal*
grouped into four general categories: I,
Digital sound-synthesis, II, Synthesizer
hardware and engineering, III,
Software systems and languages, and IV,
Perception and digital signal processing. Each section is introduced with an
"Overview" by one of the editors and the
volume as a whole contains a short but
provocative Foreword by Max Matthews.
Many articles are revised and updated
from their original state and the
anthology adds Chowning's pacesetting
article on FM sound synthesis from the
*Journal of the Audio Engineering
Society*. References at the end of each
article with a cumulative name and
subject index.

325. *RX11 Pattern Editor*. Beekman, N.Y.: Musicsoft, n.d. (for IBM PC series computers): $90.00.

> A software program which edits drum patterns. Compatible with Yamaha's *RX-11 Drum Machine*; requires MIDI hardware interface.

326. *Softsynth*. Palo Alto, Calif.: DigiDesign, n.d. (for Macintosh computers): $295.00.

> A software synthesis program for the Macintosh computer. Employs MIDI interface (hardware not included) to transmit designed waveforms.

327. *Sound Designer*. Palo Alto, Calif.: DigiDesign, n.d. (for Macintosh computers): $395.00-495.00.

> Software programs for storing, organizing, editing, and mixing digital waveforms. Compatible with *Ensoniq Mirage, E-mu Systems*, and *Sequential Prophet* samplers; require MIDI hardware interfaces.

328. *Sound Lab*. San Francisco, Calif.: Blank Software, n.d. (for Macintosh computers): $399.95.

> A software program combining digital sampling with voice editor/librarian features. Compatible with the *Ensoniq Mirage Digital Sampling Keyboard*; requires MIDI hardware interface.

329. *Soundscape Sound Digitizer*. Palo Alto, Calif.:

Mimetics, n.d. (for Amiga computers): $99.95.

A digital sound sampler in software form for Amiga computers. Contains record, edit, and play features.

330. *SYS/EX* (developed by B. Tomlyn). Berkeley, Calif.: Mix Bookshelf, n.d. (for Atari ST, Apple II series, Commodore, and IBM PC series computers): $100.00-150.00.

A series of software programs for popular microcomputers which allow you to store data from synthesizer files. Compatible with most synthesizers; require MIDI hardware interfaces.

331. *The Mimetics Data Series.* Palo Alto, Calif.: Mimetics Corporation, n.d. (for Apple and Commodore series computers): $75.00-125.00.

A series of software programs for storing, organizing, and editing waveforms. Available for Yamaha's *DX7* and *RX11*, Sequential Circuits's *SixTrack*, and Oberheim's *Drum Machine* synthesizers; require MIDI hardware interfaces.

332. Ushijima, David. "Laser Storage." *Macworld*, 3,6 (June 1986): 71.

Announcement of the first use of CD ROM in commercial application--Optical Media International's *Compact Digital Sound Storage System*, a product which stores digitized sound and synthesizer controls. Compatible with E-mu System's synthesizer, the *Emulator II.*

333. Yates, Keith. "Hi-Fi Floppy." *PC World*, 3,4 (April 1985): 190-196.

Evaluation of Compusonics *DSP-1000*, a digital recorder with PC interface. Allows sound filtering, noise removal, and other waveform alterations.

334. Yavelow, Christopher. "Digital Sampling on the Apple Macintosh: Uses of Digital Sampling for Music Applications." *Byte*, 11,6 (June 1986): 171-183.

Introduction to digital sampling techniques and the sound capabilities of the Macintosh computer. Describes and evaluates the *MacADIOS* and *MacNifty* (item 306) digitizers, *SoundCap* software and *Studio Session* editor.

335. Zimmermann, Mark. "A Beginner's Guide to Spectral Analysis, Part 1: Tiny Timesharing Music." *Byte*, 6,2 (Feb. 1981): 68-90.

Clear, non-mathematical introduction into Fourier analysis and computer-generated spectral analyzers. Combines theory, hardware diagrams, and BASIC programs in order to make a difficult subject easily understood. Bibliography.

336. Zimmermann, Mark. "A Beginner's Guide to Spectral Analysis, Part 2." *Byte*, 6,3 (March 1981): 166-198.

Assembly language program for producing two-dimensional spectral analysis.

Author Index

Abbott, G., and C. Loy,
"Programming Lan-
guages for Computer
Music Synthesis,
Performance, and
Composition," 247
Adams, Christopher,
"Sound Table: Fast
Sound Effects From
BASIC," 248
Allvin, Raynold L., *Basic
Musicianship: An
Introduction to
Music Fundamentals
with Computer Assis-
tance*, 90; "Computer-
Assisted Music In-
struction: A Look at
the Potential," 91;
"The Development of
a Computer-Assisted
Music Instruction
System to Teach

Sight-Singing and
Ear Training," 92
Anderson, J., and R.
Swirsky, "Outpost:
Atari: The State of
Atari and a Musical
Instrument to Make,"
180
Anderton, Craig, *MIDI
for Musicians*, 181;
See Moog
Arenson, M., and F.
Hofstetter, "The
GUIDO System and
the PLATO Project,"
93
Arenson, Michael, "The
Effect of a Compe-
tency-Based Comput-
er Program on the
Learning of Funda-
mental Skills in a
Music Theory Course
for Non-Majors," 94

Arveiller, J., *See* Battier
Babb, L., *See* Wittlich
Baczewski, P., *See* Killam
Bahler, Peter B., "Electronic and Computer Music: an Annotated Bibliography of Writings in English," 1
Bahn, C., *See* Dodge
Baker, Robert W. "Uncovering the C-64's CIA: New Adapter Chip Features I-O Port, Timers and More," 183
Bales, W. Kenton, "Computer-Based Instruction and Music Technology in Education," 96
Bamberger, Jeanne, "Logo Music," 97
Banes, Vince, "Audio-Frequency Analyzer: Build IBM PC Accessories to Analyze Your Stereo," 277
Barger, Victor, "Sketch the Wave," 278
Baroni, M., and L. Callegari, eds., *Musical Grammars and Computer Analysis*, 46
Bartle, Barton K., *Computer Software in Music and Music Education: A Guide*, 2

Bateman, Wayne, *Introduction to Computer Music*, 47
Battier, M., with J. Arveiller, *Musique et Informatique: Une Bibliographie Indexée*, 3
Battle, J., *See* Messick
Beauchamp, J., *See* Foerster
Bent, I., and J. Morehen, "Computers in the Analysis of Music," 48
Blombach, Ann K., "A Conceptual Framework for the Use of the Computer in Music Analysis," 49; *See* Canelos
Bonaventura, Antony P., *Making Music with Microprocessors*, 279
Boody, Charles G. "Non-Compositional Applications of the Computer to Music: An Evaluative Study of Materials Published in America Through June of 1972," 4
Boudreaux, Paul J. "Getting into Integer BASIC," 250
Bowers, D., *See* Williams
Brantley, Daniel L., "Disputed Authorship of Musical Works: A Quantitative Ap-

proach to the Attribution of the Quartets Published as Haydn's Opus 3," 50

Brook, Barry S., ed., *Musicology and the Computer: Musicology 1966-2000: A Practical Program. Three Symposia,* 5

Byrd, Donald A. "Music Notation by Computer," 51

Callegari, L., *See* Baroni

Campbell, Philip, "The Music of Digital Computers," 52

Canelos, Murphy, Blombach, and Heck, "Evaluation of Three Types of Instructional Strategy for Learner Acquisition of Intervals," 98

Carlsen, J., and D. Williams, *A Computer Annotated Bibliography: Music Research in Programmed Instruction 1952-1972,* 6

Carr, Joseph J., *Designing Microprocessor-Based Instrumentation,* 185; *Digital Interfacing with an Analog World,* 186; *Elements of Microcomputer Interfacing,* 187; *Micro-computer Interfacing Handbook: A/D & D/A,* 188

Casabona, H., and D. Frederick, "Using MIDI," 189

Chamberlin, Hal, "Advanced Real-Time Music Synthesis Techniques," 282

Ciarcia, Steve, "Sound Off," 283

Clough, John, "TEMPO: a Composer's Programming Language," 251

Clynes, Manfred, ed., *Music, Mind, and Brain: The Neuropsychology of Music,* 252

Codding, P., *See* Greenfield

Coker, Frank, "Random Music: Generate Music with a Special Twist--Just Type in These Four Little Listings," 253

Corbet, A., *See* Killam

Cowart, R., and S. Cummings, "A New Musical Revolution: What Is MIDI, and How Does Your Apple II Fit In?," 192

Crombie, David, *The New Complete Synthesizer: A Comprehensive Guide to the World of Electronic Music,* 284

Cross, Lowell, *A Bibliog-
raphy of Electronic
Music*, 9
Cummings, S., *See*
Cowart
Davis, Deta S., "Computer
Applications in
Music: A Bibliogra-
phy," 10
De Furia S., and J.
Scacciaferro, *The
Midi Implementation
Book*, 195; *The Midi
Book: Using Midi and
Related Interfaces*,
193; *The MIDI Re-
source Book*, 194; *The
MIDI System Exclus-
ive Book*, 196
De Furia, Steve, *The
Secrets of Analog to
Digital Synthesis*, 287
De Laine, Thomas H.,
"The Status of Music
Education in the
Public Schools of
Maryland, 1983-84,"
101
Dodge, C., and C. Bahn,
"Musical Fractals:
Mathematical Formu-
las Can Produce
Musical as well as
Graphic Fractals," 55
Dodge, C., and T. Jerse,
*Computer Music:
Synthesis, Composi-
tion, and Perform-
ance*, 56

Dolen, William K., "Your
Well Tempered Music
Synthesizer," 288;
"Making (Sound)
Waves with the
Macintosh," 289
Donato, Peter, "Writers
Turn Computer into
Modern Age Muse;
Composers Say Com-
puters can Up Creati-
vity once Mastered,"
11
Duncan, Danny J.,
"Practices and Stan-
dards in the Teach-
ing of Woodwind
Technique Classes in
the Music Education
Curriculum in Selec-
ted Colleges and Uni-
versities in the
United States," 104
Dworak, P., *See* Killam
Eddins, John M., "A Brief
History of Computer-
Assisted Instruction
in Music," 12; *See*
Peters
Edwards, John S., "A
Model Computer As-
sisted Information
Retrieval System in
Music Education," 105
Fink, Michael, "The
Well-Tempered
Apple," 254
Firestone, R., *See*
Krepack

Foerster, H., and J. Beauchamp, eds., *Music by Computers*, 255

Foltz, R., *See* Gross

Foltz, R., and D. Gross, "Integration of CAI into a Music Program," 106

Franklin, James L., "What's a Computer Doing in My Music Room?," 107

Frederick, D., *See* Casabona

Freiberger, P., *See* Mancini

Freff, "MIDI Gear Galore: An Endless Array of Instruments and Accessories Awaits You," 198

Fudge, Don, "Fudge It!: Tuning up Your Apple: Add Melody and a Little Charm to Your Programs with Apple Music," 256

Garvin, Mark, "Designing a Music Recorder: Here are Ways to Get Started Writing Your Own MIDI Software," 199

Gibson, Don P., "Tandy Tunes: Make Beautiful Music Together with Your Tandy 1000," 257

Glass, Jacqualine S., "The Effects of a Microcomputer-Assisted Tuning Program on Junior High School Students' Pitch Discrimination and Pitch-Matching Abilities," 108

Glines, Jeffrey, "Mac Toots Its Own Horn," 57

Gomberg, David A., "A Computer-Oriented System for Music Printing," 58

Gordon, John W., "System Architectures for Computer Music," 300

Gourlay, John S., "A Language for Music Printing," 258

Green, Gussie L., "Instructional Use of Microcomputers in Indiana Public High Schools," 109

Greenfield, D., and P. Codding, "Competency-Based Vs. Linear Computer Instruction of Music Fundamentals," 110

Grehan, R., *See* Powell, R.

Grey, John M., *An Exploration of Musical Timbre*, 301

Grijalva, Francisco J.
"Factors Influencing
Computer Use by
Music Educators in
California Indepen-
dent Elementary and
Secondary Schools,"
111
Gross, D., and R. Foltz,
"Ideas on Implemen-
tation and Evaluation
of a Music CAI
Project," 112
Gross, Dorothy S., "A Set
of Computer Pro-
grams to Aid in
Music Analysis," 59;
See Foltz
Grushcow, B., "Comput-
ers in the Private
Studio," 113
Gustafsson, Roland,
"Ensoniq Sounds,"
259
Heid, Jim, "Making
Tracks," 200;
"Musical Wares," 60
Heck, *See* Canelos
Hewlett, W., and E.
Selfridge-Field, *Di-
rectory of Computer
Assisted Research in
Musicology*, 15
Hofstetter, Fred T., "Ap-
plications of the
GUIDO System to
Aural Skills Re-
search, 1975-80," 116;
"Computer-Based
Recognition of

Perceptual Patterns
in Chord Quality
Dictation Exercises,"
117; "Evaluation of a
Competency-Based
Approach to Teach-
ing Aural Interval
Identification," 118;
"GUIDO: An Inter-
active Computer-
Based System for
Improvement of
Instruction and Re-
search in Ear-Train-
ing," 119; "Instruc-
tional Design and
Curricular Impact
of Computer-Based
Music Education,"
120; "Microelectron-
ics and Music Educa-
tion," 121; *See*
Arenson
Holland, Penny, *Looking
at Computer Sounds
and Music*, 122
Holoien, A., *See* Patton
Jackson, David L., "Hori-
zontal and Vertical
Analysis Data Extrac-
tion Using a Comput-
er Program," 61
Jainschigg, John,
"Apple Harmony,"
260
Jefferys, Douglas W.,
"Nibble Duet: Tired
of Your Apple's
Sound?" 261
Jerse, T., *See* Dodge

Katz, Robert, "Converting Pitch to Frequency," 262

Kendall, Gary S., "Theory and Application of Digital Filtering in Computer-Generated Music," 304

Killam, Baczewski, Corbet, Dworak, et al., "Research Applications in Music CAI," 126

Kirshbaum, Thomas K., "Using a Touch Tablet as an Effective, Low-Cost Input Device in a Melodic Dictation Game," 127

Kolosick, J. Timothy, "A Computer-Assisted, Set-Theoretic Investigation of Vertical Simultaneities in Selected Piano Compositions by Charles E. Ives," 62; "A Machine-Independent Data Structure for the Representation of Musical Pitch Relationships: Computer-Generated Musical Examples for CBI," 128

Kostka, Stefan M., *A Bibliography of Computer Applications in Music*, 17

Krepack, B., and R. Firestone, *Start Me Up! The Music Biz Meets the Personal Computer*, 18

Kubicky, Jay, "A MIDI Project: A MIDI Interface with Software for the IBM PC," 203

Kubitza, J., *See* Killam

Kuyper, Jon Q., "A Computer-Assisted Instruction System in Music Theory and Fundamentals," 129

Latimer, Joey, "Microtones," 263

Lavroff, Nicholas, "Roll Over Mozart," 19; "The Software Rock 'n' Roll Band," 19

Leemon, Sheldon, "More on Amiga: Software, BASIC, and IBM Compatibility," 204

Lehrman, Paul D., "Multitracking MIDI Master," 205; "Say Hello to SID: Programs for Harnessing the Music-Making Power of SID--the Commodore 64's Sound Interface Device," 206

Leibs, Albert S. "Music and the Microchip: Instruments Get User Friendly: Today's

Technology Could
Bring Out the Mozart
in You," 20
Lemons, Robert M., "The
Development and
Trial of Microcom-
puter-Assisted Tech-
niques to Supple-
ment Traditional
Training in Musical
Sightreading," 130
Levitt, David, "Pushing
the Sound Envelope:
These Programs
Make It Easier for
Musical Novices to
Make Music," 305
Levy, Steven, "MIDI Life
Crisis: Can a Colum-
nist Turn into a Rock
Superhero with a
Boost from the Mac?"
207
Lincoln, Harry B., ed.,
*The Computer and
Music*, 21
Loy, G., *See* Abbott
Mace, Scott, "Electronic
Orchestras in Your
Living Room: MIDI
Could Make 1985 the
Biggest Year Yet for
Computer Musi-
cians," 208
Malone, Thomas W.,
"What Makes Things
Fun to Learn? A
Study of Intrinsical-
ly Motivating Com-
puter Games," 133

Mancini, J., and P.
Freiberger, "Europe-
an Computer Music
Research Challenges
American Efforts," 22
Manning, Peter,
"Computers and
Music Composition,"
65; *Electronic and
Computer Music*, 23
Mason, Robert M.,
*Modern Methods of
Music Analysis Using
Computers*, 66
Massey, Howard, *The
Complete Guide to
MIDI Software*, 211
Mathews, M., and F.
Moore, "Computers
and Future Music," 24
Mathews, Miller, Moore,
et al., *The Technol-
ogy of Computer
Music*, 264
Mathews, M., *See* Risset
McClain, Larry, "A
Crescendo of
Products; Apple II
and MIDI Software,"
214
McConkey, Jim, "Report
on the Third Annual
Symposium on Small
Computers in the
Arts," 25; "The
Second Annual
Symposium on
Small Computers in
the Arts," 26

Meckley, William A., "The Development of Individualized Music Learning Sequences for Non-Handicapped, Handicapped and Gifted Learners Using the LOGO Music Version Computer Language," 134

Mefford, Michael J. "A DOS Music Generator," 265

Melby, Carol, *Computer Music Compositions of the United States*, 27

Messick, P., and J. Battle, "Build a MIDI Input for Your Casio SK-1," 216

Millar, Jana K., "The Aural Perception of Pitch-Class Set Relations: A Computer-Assisted Investigation," 138

Miller, J., *See* Mathews

Minor, David, "Music: A Buyer's Guide to Software," 224

Moog, Powell, and Anderton, eds., *Synthesizers and Computers*, 309

Moog, Powell, Rhea, Porcaro, et al., *Synthesizer Basics*, 310

Moog, Robert A., "Digital Music Synthesis: The Many Different Shapes of the Waveform of the Present," 311; "The Soundchaser Computer Music Systems," 225

Moomaw, Charles J., "A PL-1 Program for the Harmonic Analysis of Music by the Theories of Paul Hindemith and Howard Hanson," 67

Moore, F., *See* Mathews

Moorer, James A., *On the Loudness of Complex, Time-variant Tones*, 312; *On the Segmentation and Analysis of Continuous Musical Sound by Digital Computer*, 313

Morabito, Margaret, "A MIDI Musical Package: MIDI Users Sequencer/Editor," 226

Morehen, J., *See* Bent

Morgan, M., *See* Killam

Morse, Raymond W., "Use of Microcomputer Graphics to Aid in the Analysis of Music," 68

Murken, Hinrich, "Translingo," 266

Murphy, *See* Canelos

Nelson, Randolph, "A
    Graphics Text Editor
    for Music, Part 1:
    Structure of the
    Editor," 267
Orlofsky, Thomas P.,
    "Computer Music: A
    Design Tutorial," 316
Parrish, James W., "Com-
    puter Research as a
    Course of Study in
    Music Education:
    Development of an
    Exemplary Sequence
    of Teacher-Guided
    and Self-Instruction-
    al Learning Modules
    for College Music
    Majors," 143
Patton, P., and A.
    Holoien, *Computing
    in the Humanities*, 30
Pederson, Donald M.,
    "Some Techniques
    for Computer-Aided
    Analysis of Musical
    Scores," 73
Pennycook, Bruce W.
    "Computer-Music
    Interfaces: A
    Survey," 232
Perkins, Bob, "Modifi-
    cation of Celestial
    Music," 268
Peters, G., and J. Eddins,
    "Applications of
    Computers to Music
    Pedagogy, Analysis,
    and Research: A

Selected Bibliog-
    raphy," 32
Peters, G. David, "Hard-
    ware Development
    for Computer-Based
    Instruction," 144
Pierce, John R., *The
    Science of Musical
    Sound*, 319
Porcaro, S., *See* Moog
Powell, R., and R.
    Grehan, "Four MIDI
    Interfaces: MIDI
    Interfaces for
    the Commodore 64,
    IBM PC, Macintosh,
    and Apple II Family,"
    236
Powell, Roger, "The
    Challenge of Music
    Software: An Over-
    view of the Current
    State of Computers in
    Music," 33; *See* Moog
Powell, Steven, "The
    ABCs of Synthesi-
    zers," 320
Prevel, M., and F. Sallis,
    "Real-Time Genera-
    tion of Harmonic
    Progression in the
    Context of Microcom-
    puter-Based Ear
    Training." 150
Ramella, Richard,
    "Sound Advice for
    the 4/4P," 269
Raskin, Jef, "Using the
    Computer as a
    Musician's Aman-

uensis, Part 1: Fundamental Problems," 77

Reid, John W., "The Treatment of Dissonance in the Works of Guillaume Dufay, A Computer Aided Study," 78

Render, Charles R., "The Development of a Computer Program to Arrange and Print Traditional Music Notation," 79

Rhea, T., *See* Moog

Risset, C., and M. Mathews, "Analysis of Musical-Instrument Tones; with Biographical Sketches," 323

Roads, C., and J. Strawn, eds., *Foundations of Computer Music*, 324

Roads, Curtis, *Composers and the Computer*, 80; "Research in Music and Artificial Intelligence," 270

Rumery, Kenneth R., "Bringing Your Classroom Online," 156; "Computer Applications in Music Education," 157

Russell, Roberta C., "A Set of Microcomputer Programs to Aid in

the Analysis of Atonal Music," 81

Ruth, Clay, "Mockingboard Speech Update," 238

Sallis, F., *See* Prevel

Sanders, William H., "The Effect of Computer-Based Instructional Materials in a Program for Visual Diagnostic Skills Training of Instrumental Music Education Students," 158

Scacciaferro, J., *See* De Furia

Schaffer, J., *See* Wittlich

Schnebly, B. Julia, "Effects of Two Music Labeling Systems on Cognitive Processing: A Comparison of MOD 12 and Diatonic Terminology," 159

Schooley, John H., "Learning and Teaching through Technology at Home and in School; Computers Open the Door to New Ways of Mastering Music," 160

Schwaegler, David G., "A Computer-Based Trainer for Music Conducting: The

Effects of Four Feed-
back Modes," 161
Selfridge-Field, E., *See*
Hewlett
Sherborn, James W.,
"Chips and Diodes of
Microcomputers,"
163
Shrader, David L.,
"Microcomputer-
Based Teaching:
Computer-Assisted
Instruction of Music
Comes of Age," 164
Sirota, Warren, "Music
Programs for
Computers, 1," 240
Smith, David L., "Nibble
Maestro," 271
Smith, Patricia, "Com-
puters Make Music,"
82
Stein, Evan, "Use of
Computers in Folk-
lore and Folk Music:
A Preliminary
Bibliography," 36
Storey, Cheryl E., "A
Bibliography of
Computer Music," 37
Stradler, Neal, "Explor-
ing Music with
Logo," 272
Strawn, J., *See* Roads
Swearingen, Donald, "A
MIDI Recorder: Store
and Play Back Key-
board Music with
Your IBM PC," 242;
"MIDI Programming:

Processing the MPU-
401 Track Data
Stream," 243
Swirsky, Robert, *See*
Anderson
Tashjian, Thomas A.,
"Contingent Sensory
Stimulation and
Productive Vocal
Responding in
Profoundly Retarded
Multiply-Handicap-
ped Children," 166
Taylor, Jack A.,
"Computers as Music
Teachers," 167; "The
MEDICI Melodic
Dictation Computer
Program: Its Design,
Management, and
Effectiveness as
Compared to Class-
room Melodic
Notation," 168
The, Lee, "The Music
Connection: Even if
You Can't Read or
Write Music, Your
Computer Can," 38
Tjepkema, Sandra L., *A
Bibliography of
Computer Music: A
Reference for
Composers*, 39
Tubb, Phil, "Musical
Subroutines," 273
Turk, "Development of
the Music Listening
Strategy--TEMPO:
Computer Assisted

Instruction in Music Listening,"173

Upitis, Rena, "Milestones in Computer Music Instruction," 40

Ushijima, David, "Laser Storage," 332

Victor, Michele, "L'Informatique musicale," 42

Wagganer, John W., "A Comparison of Attitudes Toward Science Held by Teachers, Principals, and Parents in the State of Missouri," 174

Wallace, Robert L., "Your Sort of Computer Program!" 175

Whitney, John, "Digital Harmony: On the Complementarity of Music and Visual Art," 87

Williams, D., *See* Carlsen

Williams, D., and D. Bowers, "Designing Computer-Based Instruction for Music and the Arts," 274

Wittlich, Schaffer, and Babb, *Microcomputers and Music*, 275

Wolfe, George, "Creative Computers--Do They 'Think'?," 43

Wood, R., and P. Clements, "Systematic Evaluation Strategies for Computer-Based Music Instruction Systems," 176

Woodruff, L., *See* Killam

Yates, Keith, "Hi-fi Floppy," 333

Yavelow, Christopher, "Berklee School of Music," 177; "Digital Sampling on the Apple Macintosh: Uses of Digital Sampling for Music Applications," 334; "From Keyboard to Score: An Introduction to Music Processing and Evaluations of Six Packages that Put Your Performance on Paper," 88; "High Score," 89; "Top of the Charts: On Stage and in the Studio, the Mac Is Number One with Music Professionals," 44

Young, Jeffrey S., "Peerless Itzhak Perlman," 45

Zimmermann, Mark, "A Beginner's Guide to Spectral Analysis, Part 1," 335; "Part 2," 336.

Zimmerman, S. Scott,
    "Counting on Sixteen
    Fingers," 276
Zuk, Dorothy A., "The
    Effects of Microcom-
    puters on Children's
    Attention to Reading
    Tasks," 178

Title and Software Index

"ABCs of Synthesizers," 320

"Advanced Real-time Music Synthesis Techniques," 282

Amiga MIDI Interface, 179

"Analysis of Musical-Instrument Tones; with Biographical Sketches," 323

"Apple Harmony," 260

Apple Series MIDI Interface with Drum Sync, 182

"Applications of Computers to Music Pedagogy, Analysis, and Research: A Selected Bibliography," 32

"Applications of the GUIDO System to Aural Skills Research, 1975-80," 116

Arnold, 95

"Audio-frequency Analyzer: Build IBM PC Accessories to Analyze Your Stereo," 277

"Aural Perception of Pitch-Class Set Relations: A Computer-Assisted Investigation," 138

Basic Musicianship: An Introduction to Music Fundamentals with Computer Assistance, 90

"Beginner's Guide to Spectral Analysis, Part 1: Tiny Time-sharing Music," 335

"Beginner's Guide to Spectral Analysis, Part 2," 336

"Berklee School of
Music," 177

"Best of BIX (Bulletin
Board)," 249

*Bibliography of Computer Applications in
Music* (Kostka), 17

"Bibliography of Computer Music"
(Storey), 37

*Bibliography of Computer Music: A
Reference for Composers* (Tjepkema),
39

Bibliography of Electronic Music
(Cross), 9

"Brief History of Computer-Assisted
Instruction in
Music," 12

"Bringing Your Classroom Online," 156

"Build a MIDI Input for
Your Casio SK-1," 216

"Buyer's Guide to Music
Hardware and Software (1986); Regardless of Musical Talent, Your Family Can
Make Beautiful
Music," 184

Caged Artist Editor/Librarian Programs,
280

Casio Programmer Librarian, 281

Catch the Key, 99

"Challenge of Music
Software: An
Overview of the
Current State of Computers in Music," 33

"Chips and Diodes of
Microcomputers,"
163

Chord Mania, 100

*CODA–The New Music
Software Catalog,* 7

*Commodore 64/128 MIDI
Interface,* 190

*Commodore Series MIDI
Interface with Drum
Sync,* 188

"Comparison of Attitudes
Toward Science Held
by Teachers, Principals, and Parents
in the State of Missouri," 174

"Competency-Based Vs.
Linear Computer
Instruction of Music
Fundamentals," 110

*Complete Guide to MIDI
Software,* 211

*Composers and the
Computer,* 80

*Composers and their
Works,* 8

Computer and Music,
21

*Computer Annotated
Bibliography:
Music Research in
Programmed Instruction 1952-1972,*
6

"Computer Applications in Music Education," 157

"Computer Applications in Music: A Bibliography," 10

Computer Music Compositions of the United States, 27

"Computer Music: A Design Tutorial," 316

Computer Music: Synthesis, Composition, and Performance, 56

"Computer Research as a Course of Study in Music Education: Development of an Exemplary Sequence of Teacher-Guided and Self-Instructional Learning Modules for College Music Majors," 143

Computer Software in Music and Music Education: A Guide, 2

"Computer-Assisted Instruction System in Music Theory and Fundamentals," 129

"Computer-Assisted Music Instruction: A Look at the Potential," 91

"Computer-Assisted, Set-Theoretic Investigation of Vertical Si-multaneities in Selected Piano Compositions by Charles E. Ives," 62

"Computer-Based Instruction and Music Technology in Education," 96

"Computer-Based Recognition of Perceptual Patterns in Chord Quality Dictation Exercises," 117

"Computer-Based Trainer for Music Conducting: The Effects of Four Feedback Modes," 161

"Computer-Music Interfaces: A Survey," 232

"Computer-Oriented System for Music Printing," 58

"Computers and Future Music," 24

"Computers and Music Composition," 65

"Computers as Music Teachers," 167

"Computers in the Analysis of Music," 48

"Computers in the Private Studio," 113

"Computers Make Music," 82

Computing in the Humanities, 30

"Conceptual Framework for the Use of the

Computer in Music
Analysis," 49
ConcertWare+, 53
"Contingent Sensory
Stimulation and Pro-
ductive Vocal Re-
sponding in Pro-
foundly Retarded
Multiply-Handicap-
ped Children," 166
"Converting Pitch to
Frequency," 262
Copyist, 85
"Counting on Sixteen
Fingers," 276
"Creative Computers--Do
They 'Think'?," 43
"Crescendo of Products;
Apple II and MIDI
Software," 214
*CZ Patch Editor/Librar-
ian,* 285
CZ Rider, 286
*Deluxe Music Construc-
tion Set,* 54
"Designing a Music Re-
corder: Here Are
Ways to Get Started
Writing Your Own
MIDI Software," 199
"Designing Computer-
Based Instruction for
Music and the Arts,"
274
"Designing Micropro-
cessor-Based Instru-
mentation," 185
"Development and Trial
of Microcomputer-
Assisted Techniques

to Supplement Tra-
ditional Training in
Musical Sightread-
ing," 130
"Development of a Com-
puter Program to Ar-
range and Print Tra-
ditional Music Nota-
tion," 79
"Development of a Com-
puter-Assisted Music
Instruction System to
Teach Sight-Singing
and Ear Training,"
92
"Development of Indi-
vidualized Music
Learning Sequences
for Non-Handicap-
ped, Handicapped
and Gifted Learners
Using the LOGO Music
Version Computer
Language, 134
"Development of the
Music Listening
Strategy--TEMPO:
Computer Assisted
Instruction in Music
Listening," 173
Diatonic Chords, 102
*Digital Harmony: On the
Complementarity of
Music and Visual Art,*
87
*Digital Interfacing with
an Analog World,* 186
"Digital Music Synthesis:
The Many Different
Shapes of the Wave-

form of the Present,"
311
"Digital Sampling on the
Apple Macintosh:
Uses of Digital Samp-
ling for Music Appli-
cations," 334
*Directory of Computer
Assisted Research in
Musicology,* 15
"Disputed Authorship of
Musical Works: A
Quantitative Ap-
proach to the Attri-
bution of the Quar-
tets Published as
Haydn's Opus 3," 50
Doremi, 103
"DOS Music Generator,"
265
*Dr. T'S Model T-MIDI
Interface,* 197
DX Android, 290
DX Connect, 291
*DX Patch Editor/Librar-
ian,* 292
*DX-1 Sound Sampling
System,* 293
DX-TX Support Programs,
294
DX-TX-LP, 295
DXLIB, 296
"Effect of a Competency-
Based Computer Pro-
gram on the Learn-
ing of Fundamental
Skills in a Music
Theory Course for
Non-Majors," 94

"Effect of Computer-
Based Instructional
Materials in a Pro-
gram for Visual Di-
agnostic Skills Train-
ing of Instrumental
Music Education Stu-
dents," 158
"Effects of a Microcom-
puter-Assisted Tun-
ing Program on Ju-
nior High School
Students' Pitch Dis-
crimination and
Pitch-Matching
Abilitites," 108
"Effects of Microcom-
puters on Children's
Attention to Reading
Tasks," 178
"Effects of Two Music
Labeling Systems on
Cognitive Proces-
sing: A Comparison
of MOD 12 and Dia-
tonic Terminology,"
159
*Electronic and Computer
Music* (Manning), 23
"Electronic and Comput-
er Music: an Anno-
tated Bibliography of
Writings in English"
(Bahler), 1
"Electronic Orchestras
in Your Living
Room: MIDI Could
Make 1985 the Big-
gest Year Yet for

Computer Musi-
cians," 208
*Elements of Microcom-
puter Interfacing,*
187
"Ensoniq Sounds," 259
Envelope Construction,
297
Envelope Shaper, 298
"European Computer
Music Research
Challenges American
Efforts," 22
"Evaluation of a Compe-
tency-Based Ap-
proach to Teaching
Aural Interval Iden-
tification," 118
"Evaluation of Three
Types of Instruction-
al Strategy for
Learner Acquisition
of Intervals," 98
*Exploration of Musical
Timbre,* 301
"Explore Temperament:
The MIRAGE Multi-
Temperament Disk,"
299
"Exploring Music with
Logo," 272
"Factors Influencing
Computer Use by
Music Educators in
California Indepen-
dent Elementary and
Secondary Schools,"
111
*Foreign Instrument
Names,* 13

*Foundations of Computer
Music,* 324
"Four MIDI Interfaces:
MIDI Interfaces for
the Commodore 64,
IBM PC, Macintosh,
and Apple II Family,"
236
"Fudge It!: Tuning Up
Your Apple: Add
Melody and a Little
Charm to Your Pro-
grams with Apple
Music," 256
General Music Terms, 14
"Getting into Integer
BASIC," 250
"Graphics Text Editor for
Music, Part 1:
Structure of the
Editor," 267
*GUIDO Ear-Training
System,* 169
"GUIDO System and the
PLATO Project,"
93
"GUIDO: An Interactive
Computer-Based Sys-
tem for Improve-
ment of Instruction
and Research in
Ear-Training," 119
"Hardware Development
for Computer-Based
Instruction," 144
Harmonious Dictator,
114
Harmony Drills: Set I,
115
"Hi-Fi Floppy," 333

"High Score," 89
Hippo 8-Bit Audio Sampler, 302
"Horizontal and Vertical Analysis Data Extraction Using a Computer Program," 61
Hybrid Arts DX Editor/Librarian, 303
"Ideas on Implementation and Evaluation of a Music CAI Project," 112
IFM Interface, 201
"Informatique musicale" (Musical Data Processing), 42
"Instructional Design and Curricular Impact of Computer-Based Music Education," 120
"Instructional Use of Microcomputers in Indiana Public High Schools," 109
"Integration of CAI into a Music Program," 106
Interval Mania, 123
Introduction to Computer Music, 47
Italian Terms, 16
Jazz Dictator, 124
Key Signature Drills, 125
Keyboard Controlled Sequencer, 202
"Keyboard to Score: An Introduction to Music Processing and Evaluations of Six Packages that Put Your Performances on Paper," 88
"Language for Music Printing," 258
"Laser Storage," 332
Leadsheeter, 63
"Learning & Teaching through Technology at Home and in School; Computers Open the Door to New Ways of Mastering Music," 160
"Logo Music," 97
Looking at Computer Sounds and Music, 122
"Mac Toots Its Own Horn," 57
MacFace MIDI Interface, 209
"Machine-Independent Data Structure for the Representation of Musical Pitch Relationships: Computer-Generated Musical Examples for CBI," 128
Macintosh MIDI Interface, 210
MacMusic, 64
Macnifty Audio Digitizer, 306
MacVoice, 131
Magic Musical Balloon Game, 132

"Making (Sound) Waves
    with the Macintosh,"
    289
*Making Music with
    Microprocessors*, 279
"Making Tracks," 200
Master Tracks Pro v1.1,
    212
Masterpiece, 213
"MEDICI Melodic Dicta-
    tion Computer Pro-
    gram: Its Design,
    Management, and
    Effectiveness as
    Compared to Class-
    room Melodic No-
    tation," 168
MegaTrack (XL) v2.1, 215
Melodious Dictator, 135
Melody Race, 136
Micro Brass Series (for
    trumpet, horn, bari-
    one, and tuba), 137
*Microcomputer Inter-
    facing Handbook:
    A/D & D/A*, 188
"Microcomputer-Based
    Teaching: Computer-
    Assisted Instruction
    of Music Comes of
    Age," 164
*Microcomputers and
    Music*, 275
"Microelectronics and
    Music Education," 121
"Microtones," 263
*Midi Book: Using
    Midi and Related
    Interfaces*, 193
MIDI for Musicians, 181

"MIDI Gear Galore: An
    Endless Array of
    Instruments and
    Accessories Awaits
    You," 198
*Midi Implementation
    Book*, 195
"MIDI Life Crisis: Can a
    Columnist Turn into
    a Rock Superhero
    with a Boost from the
    Mac?," 207
"MIDI Musical Package:
    MIDI Users Sequen-
    cer/Editor," 226
MIDI Pro Tool Kit, 217
"MIDI Programming:
    Processing the MPU-
    401 Track Data
    Stream," 243
"MIDI Project: A MIDI
    Interface with Soft-
    ware for the IBM PC,"
    203
"MIDI Recorder: Store
    and Play Back Key-
    board Music with
    Your IBM PC," 242
MIDI Resource Book,
    194
*MIDI System Exclusive
    Book*, 196
MIDI Track III, 218
*MIDI/4 and MIDI/8
    PLUS*, 219
*MIDIMAC Patch Librar-
    ians*, 307
MIDIMac Sequencer
    v3.0, 220
MIDIMate Interface, 221

MIDIMerge, 222
MIF-MIDI Interface, 223
"Milestones in Computer
Music Instruction,"
40
Mimetics Data Series,
331
*Mirage and Prophet
Sonic Editors,* 308
"Mockingboard Speech
Update," 238
Mode Drills, 139
"Model Computer As-
sisted Information
Retrieval System in
Music Education,"
105
*Modern Methods of
Music Analysis Using
Computers,* 66
"Modification of Celesti-
al Music," 268
"More on Amiga: Soft-
ware, BASIC, and IBM
Compatibility," 204
*MPU-401 MIDI Proces-
sing Unit,* 227
*Multitracking MIDI
Master,* 205
"Music & the Microchip:
Instruments Get User
Friendly: Today's
Technology Could
Bring Out the Mozart
in You," 20
Music Analysis System,
86
Music by Computers, 255
Music Composer, 69

"Music Connection:
Even if You Can't
Read or Write Music,
Your Computer Can,"
38
Music Detective, 170
*Music in Theory and
Practice,* Volumes I
and II, 3rd edition,
140
"Music Notation by Com-
puter," 51
"Music of Digital Com-
puters," 52
*Music Processing
System,* 228
"Music Programs for
Computers, 1," 240
Music Shop-MIDI, 245
Music Symbols, 28
Music Terminology, 29
*Music, Mind, and Brain:
The Neuropsycholo-
gy of Music,* 252
"Music: A Buyer's Guide
to Software," 224
"Musical Fractals: Math-
ematical Formulas
Can Produce Musical
as well as Graphic
Fractals," 55
*Musical Grammars and
Computer Analysis,*
46
"Musical Subroutines,"
273
"Musical Wares," 60
Musicland, 141
*Musicology and the
Computer: Musicol-*

ogy 1966-2000: A Practical Program. Three Symposia, 5
MusicPrinter v.2.0, 70
MusicSoft Drum Machine Data Managers, 314
MusicType, 71
MusicWorks, 72
Musique et Informatique: Une Bibliographie Indexée, 3
Name It: Kids' Classics, 142
New Complete Synthesizer: A Comprehensive Guide to the World of Electronic Music, 284
"New Musical Revolution: What Is MIDI, and How Does Your Apple II Fit In?," 192
"Nibble Duet: Tired of Your Apple's Sound?," 261
"Nibble Maestro," 271
"Non-Compositional Applications of the Computer to Music: An Evaluative Study of Materials Published in America Through June of 1972," 4
Oasis, 315
On the Loudness of Complex, Time-Variant Tones, 312

On the Segmentation and Analysis of Continuous Musical Sound by Digital Computer, 313
Opcode Macintosh [Plus] Interface, 229
Opcode Studio Plus II Interface, 230
"Outpost: Atari: The State of Atari and a Musical Instrument to Make," 180
Passport MIDI Voice Librarians, 317
Patch Master, 318
PC-MIDI Card, 231
"Peerless Itzhak Perlman," 45
Performer v2.3, 233
Personal Composer v2.0, 74
Personal Musician, 234
Peter and the Wolf, 31
Pick the Pitch, 145
Pitch Drills With Accidentals, 146
Pitch Drills Without Accidentals, 147
Pitch Duel, 148
Pitch-u-lation, 149
"PL-1 Program for the Harmonic Analysis of Music by the Theories of Paul Hindemith and Howard Hanson," 67
Polywriter, 75
Polywriter Utilities, 235

"Practices and Standards in the Teaching of Woodwind Technique Classes in the Music Education Curriculum in Selected Colleges and Universities in the United States," 104

PRO-16 and PRO-24, 237

Pro-Creator, 321

Proceedings of the International Computer Music Conference, 34

Professional Composer v2.2, 76

"Programming Languages for Computer Music Synthesis, Performance, and Composition," 247

PROLIB, 322

ProMIDI Studio System, 246

"Pushing the Sound Envelope: These Programs Make it Easier for Musical Novices to Make Music," 305

"Random Music: Generate Music with a Special Twist--Just Type in these Four Little Listings," 253

"Real-Time Generation of Harmonic Progression in the Context of Microcomputer-Based Ear Training," 150

"Report on the Third Annual Symposium on Small Computers in the Arts," 25

"Research Applications in Music CAI," 126

"Research in Music and Artificial Intelligence," 270

Rhythm Drills, 151

Rhythm Machine, 152

Rhythm Write, 153

Rhythmaticity, 154

Rhythmic Dictator, 155

"Roll over Mozart," 19

RX11 Pattern Editor, 325

"Say Hello to SID: Programs for Harnessing the Music-making Power of SID--the Commodore 64's Sound Interface Device," 206

Science of Musical Sound, 319

Sebastian II, 162

"Second Annual Symposium on Small Computers in the Arts," 26

Secrets of Analog to Digital Synthesis, 287

Sequencer Plus v2.0, 239

"Set of Computer Programs to Aid in Music Analysis," 59

"Set of Microcomputer Programs to Aid in

the Analysis of
Atonal Music," 81
Sir William Wrong Note,
165
"Sketch the Wave," 278
Softsynth, 326
"Software Rock 'n' Roll
Band," 19
Sonata v1.6, 83
Songwright+, 84
"Sound Advice for the
4/4P," 269
Sound Designer, 327
Sound Lab, 328
"Sound Off," 283
"Sound Table: Fast Sound
Effects From BASIC,"
248
"Soundchaser Computer
Music Systems,"
225
*Soundscape ProMIDI
Studio,* 241
*Soundscape Sound Digi-
tizer,* 329
*Standard Instrument
Names,* 35
*Start Me Up! The Music
Biz Meets the Per-
sonal Computer,* 18
"Status of Music Educa-
tion in the Public
Schools of Maryland,
1983-84," 101
Synthesizer Basics, 310
SYS/EX, 330
"System Architectures
for Computer Music,"
300

"Systematic Evaluation
Strategies for Com-
puter-Based Music
Instruction Systems,"
176
*Sythesizers and Com-
puters,* 309
"Tandy Tunes: Make
Beautiful Music
Together with
Your Tandy 1000,"
257
"Techniques for Com-
puter-Aided Analysis
of Musical Scores,"
73
*Technology of Computer
Music,* 264
"TEMPO: a Composer's
Programming Lan-
guage," 251
Texture v2.0, 244
"Theory and Application
of Digital Filtering in
Computer-Generated
Music," 304
Theory Sampler, 171
Toney Listens to Music,
172
"Top of the Charts: On
Stage and in the Stu-
dio, the Mac Is Num-
ber One with Music
Professionals," 44
Translingo, 266
"Treatment of Disso-
nance in the Works
of Guillaume Dufay,
A Computer Aided
Study," 78

"Uncovering the C-64's CIA: New Adapter Chip Features I-O Port, Timers and More," 183

"US Festival," 41

"Use of Computers in Folklore and Folk Music: A Preliminary Bibliography," 36

"Use of Microcomputer Graphics to Aid in the Analysis of Music," 68

"Using a Touch Tablet as an Effective, Low-Cost Input Device in a Melodic Dictation Game," 127

Using MIDI, 189

"Using the Computer as a Musician's Amanuensis, Part 1: Fundamental Problems," 77

"Well-Tempered Apple," 254

"What Makes Things Fun to Learn? A Study of Intrinsically Motivating Computer Games," 133

"What's a Computer Doing in My Music Room?," 107

"Writers Turn Computer into Modern Age Muse; Composers Say Computers Can Up

Creativity Once Mastered," 11

"Your Sort of Computer Program!," 175

"Your Well Tempered Music Synthesizer," 288

Appendix A:
Journals which Regularly Contain
Articles on
Microcomputers and Music

The journals below offer reqularly appearing articles, code, and advertising information concerning microcumputer applications in music. You should not expect to find these in your local library; they are trade journals and are not, as a rule, purchased by public or research facilities.

Joseph Puccio of the Library of Congress, Washington, D.C., has compiled a useful guide "Computer Periodicals Currently Received in the Library of Congress." This pamphlet was first published in July of 1985 and is currently undergoing revisions; it may be ordered from The Library of Congress Serial and Government Publications Division, Periodical Section (LC, Washington, D.C.). Puccio's guide offers several hundred listings of magazines devoted to microcomputer applications in all fields.

Microcomputer journals have a tendency to change their titles; consequently, alternate and former title names have been supplied. The only organ to devote itself specifically to music applications is *The Computer Music Journal*, a publication of high academic standards which is worthy of special attention.

Ordering and circulation information concerning these specific journals has been gathered from *Ulrich's International Periodicals Directory: A Classified Guide to Current Periodicals, Foreign and Domestic, 1986-1987* (New York: R.R. Bowker, 25th ed., 1986).

80 Micro: the Magazine for TRS-80 Users. 1980- (monthly): $24.97. C W Communications, Box 981, Farmingdale, N.Y., 11737, tele.: 603/924-9471. Editor: Eric Maloney; circulation: 101,000. ISSN: 0744-7868.

Formerly: *Hot CoCo; 80 Microcomputing*

A+; the Independent Guide to Apple II and Macintosh Computing. 1983- (monthly): $24.97. Ziff-Davis Publishing Co., Computer Publications Division, One Park Ave., New York, N.Y., 10016, tele.: 212/503-3500. Editor: Maggie Canon; circulation: 200,000. ISSN: 0740-1590.

Formerly: *A+ For Apple Computing*

Antic: The Atari Resource. 1982- (monthly): $3.00 per number. Antic Publishing, 524 2nd Street, San Francisco, Calif., 94107, tele.: 415/957-0886. Editor: James Capparell; circulation: 100,000. ISSN: 0745-2527.

Byte: the Small Systems Journal. 1975- (monthly): $21.00. McGraw-Hill, Inc., Box 590, Martinsville, N.J., 08836, tele.: 603/924-9281. Editor: Philip Lemmons; circulation: 399,000. ISSN: 0360-5280.

Call A.P.P.L.E. 1978- (monthly): $21.00. Apple

Pugetsound Program Library Exchange, 290 S.W. 43rd, Renton, Wash., 98055-4936, tele.: 206/251-5222. Editor: Don Elman; circulation: 30,000. ISSN: 8755-4909.

Classroom Computer Learning; the Leading Magazine of Electronic Education. 1980- (monthly): $22.50. Peter Li, Inc., 2451 East River Rd., Dayton, Ohio, 45439, tele.: 513/294-5785. Editor: Holly Brady; circulation: 80,000. ISSN: 0746-4223.

Formerly: *Classroom Computer News*

Commodore Microcomputers. 1981- (bimonthly): $15.00. Commodore Business Machines, Inc., Box 651, Holmes, Pa., 19043, tele.: 215/431-9100. Editor: Diane Lebold, circulation: 165,000.

Formerly: *Commodore: the Microcomputer Magazine*

Compute!: the Leading Magazine of Home, Educational, and Recreational Computing. 1979- (monthly): $24.00. Compute! Publications, Inc., Box 10954, Des Moines, Iowa, 50340, tele.: 919/275-9809. Editor: Tom Halfhill; circulation: 350,000. ISSN: 0194-357X.

Formerly: *Home and Education Computing, P.E.T. Gazette*

Computer Music Journal. 1977- (quarterly): $53.00 (inds., 26.00). MIT Press, 28 Carleton St., Cambridge Mass., 02142, tele.: 617/253-2889. Editor: Curtis Roads; circulation: 3,000. ISSN: 0148-9267.

Computing Teacher. 1979- (monthly): $21.50.
International Council for Computers in Education,
1787 Agate, University of Oregon, Eugene, Ore.,
97403, tele.: 503/686-4429. By editorial board;
circulation: 17,000. ISSN: 0278-9175.

*Creative Computing; Magazine of Personal
Computer Applications and Software.* 1974-
(monthly): no longer available. Ziff-Davis
Publishing Co., One Park Ave., New York, N.Y., 10016.
ISSN: 0097-8140.

Dr. Dobb's Journal of Software Tools. 1976-
(monthly): $25.00. M & T Publishing Inc., 2464
Embarcadero Way, Palo Alto, Calif., 94303, tele.:
415/424-0600. Editor: Michael Swaines; circulation:
60,000.

Formerly: *Dr. Dobb's Journal: Software
Tools for Advanced Programmers*; others.

Electronic Learning. 1981- (8/yr.): $19.95.
Scholastic, Inc., 730 Broadway, New York, N.Y.,
10003, tele.: 212/505-3000. Editor: Robert Burroughs;
circulation: 58,000. ISSN: 0278-3258.

Family [and Home Office] Computing. 1983-
(monthly): $19.97. Scholastic, Inc., 730 Broadway,
New York, N.Y., 10003, tele.: 212/505-3580. Editor:
Claudia Cohl; circulation: 410,000. ISSN: 0738-6079.

Home Computer Magazine. 1981- (10.yr.): $25.00.
Emerald Valley Publishing Co., Box 5537, 1500 Valley
River Dr., Ste., 250, Eugene, Ore., 97401, tele.:

503/485-8796, Editor: Gary Kaplan; circulation: 250,000. ISSN: 0747-055X.

Formerly: *99'er Home Computer Magazine*

inCider. 1983- (monthly): $24.97. C W Communications, Box 911, Farmingdale, N.Y., 11737, tele.: 603-924-9471. Editor: Debbie de Peyster; circulation, 105,000. ISSN: 0740-0101.

InfoWorld; the Personal Computing Weekly. 1979- (weekly): $31.00. C W Communications, Inc., Circulation Department, 375 Cochituate Rd., Box 837, Framingham, Mass., 01701, tele.: 415/328-4602. Editor: James Fawcette; circulation: 125,000. ISSN: 0199-6649.

Formerly: *Intelligent Machines Journal*

Journal of Computer-Based Instruction. 1974- (quarterly): $36.00. Association for the Development of Computer-Based Instructional Systems, Western Washington University, Bellingham, Wash., 98225, tele.: 206/676-2860. Editor: Allen Avner; circulation, 2,300. ISSN: 0098-597X.

Keyboard; for all Keyboard Players. 1975- (monthly): $19.95. G P I Publications, 20085 Stevens creek, Cupertino, Calif., 95014, tele.: 408/446-1105. Editor: Dominic Milano; circulation: 68,000. ISSN: 0730-0158.

Formerly: *Contemporary Keyboard*

Macworld. 1984- (monthly): $30.00. P C World

Communications, Inc., Box 20300, Bergenfield, N.J., 07621, tele.: 415/861-3861. Editor: Kearney Rietmann; circulation: 150,000. ISSN: 0741-8647.

Music Educators Journal. 1914- (9/yr.): $25.00. Music Educators National Conference, Center for Educational Associations, 1902 Association Dr., Reston, Va., 22091, tele.: 703-860-4000. Editor: Rebecca Taylor; circulation: 60,000. ISSN: 0027-4321.

Nibble: the Reference for Apple Computing, 1980- (monthly): $26.95. Micro-Sparc, Inc., 45 Winthrop St., Concord, Mass., 01742, tele.: 617/371-1660. Editor: Mike Harvey; circulation: 75,000. ISSN: 0734-3795.

P C M; the Personal Computer Magazine for Tandy Computer Users. 1983- (monthly): $28.00. Falsoft, Inc., Falsoft Bldg., Box 385, Prospect, Ky., 40059, tele.: 502/228-4492. Editor: Lawrence Falk; circulation: 10,000.

Formerly: *Portable Computing*

P C Week. 1983- (weekly): $120.00. Ziff-Davis Publishing Co., 381 Elliot St., Newton, Mass., 02164, tele.: 617/449-6520. Editor: advisory board, circulation: 112,000. ISSN: 0740-1604.

P C World; the Comprehensive Guide to IBM PCs and Compatibles. 1982- (monthly): $23.75. P C World Communications, Inc., Box 6700, Bergenfield, N.J., 07621, tele.: 415/861-3861. Editor: Harry Miller; circulation: 277,000. ISSN: 0737-8939.

P C: the Independent Guide to IBM Personal Computers (=PC Magazine). 1982- (22/yr.): $34.97. Ziff-Davis Publishing Co., Box 2443, Boulder, Colo., 80321, tele.: 212/503-3500. Editor: Bill Machrone, circulation: 300,000. ISSN: 0745-2500.

Personal Computer World. 1978- (monthly): £10. V N U Business Publications Ltd., 62 Oxford St., London W1A 2HG, England. Editor: Jane Bird; circulation: 66,000. ISSN: 0142-0232.

Personal Computing. 1976- (monthly): $18.00. Hayden Publishing Co., Inc., Box 2942, Boulder, Colo., 80322, tele.: 201/393-6000. Editor: Charles Martin; circulation: 550,000.

Formerly: *Personal Computing Plus; Personal Software Magazine*

Popular Computing. 1979- (monthly): $15.00. McGraw-Hill Information Systems Co., Box 307, Martinsville, N.J., 08836, tele.: 603/924-9281. Editor: Pamela Clark; circulation: 242,000. ISSN: 0279-4721.

Formerly: *On Computing*

Practical Computing. 1979 (monthly): $47.00. Electrical-Electronic Press Ltd., Quadrant House, The Quadrant, Surrey SM2 5AS, England. Editor: Glyn Moody; circulation: 52,000. ISSN: 0141-5433.

Appendix B:
A Checklist of Twenty Books
for the
Small Music Library

The following books have been selected because they provide universal coverage of the subject matter or because they examine specialized topics particularly well. No claim is made for inclusiveness in such a brief list; however these sources will supply the small library with a corpus of useful texts in all six of the subject indexes presented above. As of late 1987, these books are known to be in print.

Small libraries may also wish to subscribe to at least one computer oriented journal and the logical choice is *The Computer Music Journal* cited in the previous appendix.

7. *Coda–The New Music Software Catalog.* Owatonna, Maine: Wenger Corporation, 1986. 160pp. $4.00.

15. Hewlett, W., and E. Selfridge-Field. *Directory of Computer-Assisted Research in Musicology.* Menlo Park, Calif.: Center for Computer Assisted Research in the Humanities, 1987. 151pp.

18. Krepack, B., and R. Firestone. *Start Me Up! The Music Biz Meets the Personal Computer.* Van Nuys, Calif.: Media Press, 1986. xvii, 171pp. 0961644605. $12.95.

23. Manning, Peter. *Electronic and Computer Music.* Oxford: Clarendon Press, 1985. 291pp. 0193119188. $29.95.

39. Tjepkema, Sandra L. *A Bibliography of Computer Music: A Reference for Composers.* Iowa City, Iowa: University of Iowa Press, 1981. xvii, 276pp. 0877451109.

56. Dodge, C., and T. Jerse. *Computer Music: Synthesis, Composition, and Performance.* New York: Schirmer Books, 1985. xi, 383pp. 002873100X.

66. Mason, Robert M. *Modern Methods of Music Analysis Using Computers.* Peterborough, N.H.: Schoolhouse Press, 1985. 299pp. 0961566906. $39.50.

80. Roads, Curtis, ed. *Composing and the Computer* (The Computer Music and Digital Audio Series). Los Alto, Calif.: William Kaufmann, Inc., 1984. xxi, 201pp. 0865760853.

87. Whitney, John. *Digital Harmony: On the Complementarity of Music and Visual Art.* Peterborough, N.H.: Byte Books by McGraw-Hill, 1980. 235pp. 007070015X. $21.95.

122. Holland, Penny. *Looking at Computer Sounds and*

Music (An Easy-Read Computer Activity Book). New York: Franklin Watts, 1986. 32pp. 0531100979.

187. Carr, Joseph J. *Elements of Microcomputer Interfacing*. Reston, Va.: Prentice-Hall, 1984. x, 387pp. 0835917053.

193. De Furia, S., and J. Scacciaferro. *The Midi Book: Using Midi and Related Interfaces*. Rutherford, N.J.: Third Earth Productions, Inc., 1986. 95pp. 0881885142. $14.95.

252. Clynes, Manfred, ed. *Music, Mind, and Brain: The Neuropsychology of Music*. New York: Plenum Press, 1982. xii, 430pp. 0306409089.

264. Mathews, M., J. Miller, et al. *The Technology of Computer Music*. Cambridge, Mass.: MIT Press, 1969/1974. 188pp. 0262130505.

275. Wittlich, Schaffer, and Babb. *Microcomputers and Music*. Englewood Cliffs, N.J.: Prentice-Hall, 1986. xiii, 321pp. 0135805155.

284. Crombie, David. *The New Complete Synthesizer: A Comprehensive Guide to the World of Electronic Music*. New York: Omnibus Press, 1986. 112pp. 0711907013. $12.95.

301. Grey, John M. *An Exploration of Musical Timbre* (Center for Computer Research in Music and Acoustics, STAN-M-2). Palo Alto, Calif.: Department

of Music: Stanford University, 1975. 133pp. 76-377790.

309. Moog, Powell, and Anderton, eds. *Synthesizers and Computers* (Keyboard Synthesizer Library). Milwaukee, Wis.: Hal Leonard Publishing Corp., 1985. iv, 129pp. 0881882917. $9.95.

319. Pierce, John R. *The Science of Musical Sound* (Scientific American Library). New York: Scientific American Books, Inc., 1983. xii, 242pp. 0716715082.

324. Roads, C., and J. Strawn, eds. *Foundations of Computer Music*. Cambridge, Mass.: MIT Press, 1985. xiii, 712pp. 0262181142.